JIMI HENDRIX

BY JOHN ROBERTSON

Copyright © 1995 Omnibus Press (A Division of Book Sales Limited)

Edited by Chris Charlesworth
Cover & Book designed by 4i Limited
Picture research by Nikki Russell

ISBN: 0.7119.4304.4 Order No: OP47739

Exclusive Distributors
Book Sales Limited, 8/9 Frith Street, London W1V 5TZ, UK.
Music Sales Corporation, 257 Park Avenue South, New York, NY 10010, USA.
Music Sales Pty Limited, 120 Rothschild Avenue, Rosebery, NSW 2018, Australia.

To the Music Trade only:
Music Sales Limited, 8/9 Frith Street, London W1V 5TZ, UK.

Photos courtesy of Andre Csillag, Harry Goodwin & Barry Plummer.

Every effort has been made to trace the copyright holders of the photographs in this book but one or two were unreachable. We would be grateful if the photographers concerned would contact us.

Printed in the United Kingdom by Ebenezer Baylis & Son, Worcester

A catalogue record for this book is available from the British Library.

CONTENTS

INTRODUCTION

Jimi Hendrix's 'official' recording career lasted almost exactly four years. The first two were marked by a Herculean work-rate and awe-inspiring artistic progression. The last two were a morass of indecision, lack of direction, and encroaching depression.

When he died in September 1970, all the talk was about what might have been. In his own mind, though, Jimi had long regarded himself as a failure, unable to build on the creative and commercial success of his first three albums – unable, in fact, even to complete a single studio project since then.

As Bob Dylan sang, 'Death Is Not The End' – a maxim that certainly applies to Hendrix's release schedule. In fact, his untimely demise was only the beginning of a long-term exploitation exercise that has hurled literally scores of albums into the shops since 1970. The initial rush to cash in on his death was only to be expected, but the recent saturation of the market (coinciding neatly with the CD boom) is proof of Hendrix's catch-all appeal to several generations of rock fans, from his original admirers to those who were born years after he choked to death in a London hotel.

There are currently well over 100 Jimi Hendrix CDs in the shops, plus twice as many again on the underground bootleg circuit. The purpose of this book is to steer listeners new and old through the chaos that awaits anyone who checks out the Hendrix rack in their local megastore. Faced with the profusion of digital revamps, callous repackages and deliberate rip-offs, even the most hardened rock consumer can be forgiven for needing a friendly guide.

The book is divided into four main sections. After a brief chronology of Jimi's life and career, and a thumbnail sketch of the main protagonists in his story, Section 1 details the Official Albums – the mere handful of records released in Jimi's lifetime.

Section 2 covers the Posthumous Albums, but only those which have been released by, or with the co-operation of, the executors and trustees of his Estate. As in the first section, these albums are listed in the order of their original release. An appendix to this section details worldwide CD singles.

Section 3 surveys the plethora of Unofficial Albums which litter the record stores of the world – restricted solely to CDs, in the interests of space and sanity. These cover everything from Hendrix interviews to haphazard collections of his pre-fame work as a session guitarist, via illicitly obtained live tapes and unsupervised rehashes of the Official Albums. The one thing they have in common is that they all are, or have been, on sale in legitimate record stores in Britain and America, and have therefore (often only by a legal loophole) escaped the 'bootleg' tag.

Finally, the book ends with Section 4 – a brief listing of Jimi's guest appearances with other artists, plus a guide to their availability on CD.

Even this listing of 'official' CDs scarcely touches the surface of Jimi Hendrix's recording career. Collectors and fans have access to an underground network which supplies them with hundreds of hours of officially unreleased concert tapes, studio out-takes, jam sessions and interviews. An inveterate chronicler of his own musical dabblings, Hendrix kept tapes of his composing stints, rehearsals and after-hours collaborations with fellow club-goers.

Being prolific is obviously not a substitute for being creative. No doubt a die-hard fan of James Last could fill a wardrobe or two with concert tapes and albums. What turns the obsession of the collector into the search for the Holy Grail is Hendrix's almost superhuman proficiency as a guitarist, and his endless quest for artistic innovation. As a musician, Jimi pioneered a form of expression that encompassed everything the technicians could throw at him, and burst through all known genre barriers. As an artist, he had a vision of a union of experimental music, poetic lyrics and spiritual awareness that has inspired generations of musicians and writers.

Champions of rock, jazz, soul, blues and the avant-garde have all tried to claim Hendrix as their own. He remains the most complete musician ever to have performed rock'n'roll – and the irony is that much of his reputation is based on music which he would never have allowed us to hear if he had lived. His legacy, as documented in this book, proves that four years are quite long enough for a genius to re-make the history of music in his own image.

John Robertson, December 1994

CHRONOLOGY

27 NOVEMBER 1942 Johnny Allen Hendrix is born in Seattle, Washington, the son of Al Hendrix and Lucille Jeter, who married on 31st March in this year. Hendrix is originally raised by his mother, while his father is in the Services. The couple rarely live together with their son.

11 SEPTEMBER 1946 Al Hendrix changes his son's name to James Marshall Hendrix.

13 JANUARY 1948 Jimi's brother Leon is born in Seattle.

MID-1949 A third brother, Joseph Allen Hendrix, is also born in Seattle. Around this time, Jimi and Leon are sent to Vancouver to live with Al's sister and her husband. They return to Seattle in 1950.

27 SEPTEMBER 1950 Jimi's sister Cathy Ira Hendrix is born in Seattle.

17 DECEMBER 1951 Al and Lucille Hendrix are divorced. Jimi, Leon and Joseph live with their father, though Joseph soon moves elsewhere, and Leon is often fostered out during the 1950s.

2 FEBRUARY 1958 Jimi's mother Lucille dies in Seattle: neither he nor his father attend the funeral.

AUTUMN 1958 Al Hendrix gives Jimi a ukelele, inspiring him to buy a $5 guitar later in the year. Jimi soon joins his first group, The Velvetones, playing acoustic guitar.

SUMMER 1959 Al purchases an electric guitar for his son, allowing Jimi to join another band, The Rocking Kings – with whom he makes his live début later that year.

SUMMER 1960 The Rocking Kings evolve into Thomas & The Tomcats.

31 OCTOBER 1960 Jimi leaves high school without graduating.

31 MAY 1961 After several run-ins with the Seattle police, Jimi enlists in the US Army, and begins his basic training.

31 OCTOBER 1961 Jimi joins the 101st Airborne Division, where he undergoes parachute training.

2 JULY 1962 After breaking his ankle in his 26th parachute jump, Jimi is invalided out of the army.

OCTOBER 1962 With his army buddy Billy Cox, Jimi starts work as a musician-for-hire in Nashville clubs.

DECEMBER 1962 Jimi joins the mixed-race R&B band Bobby Taylor and The Vancouvers, who later sign to Motown.

MARCH 1963 Back in Nashville, Hendrix and Cox form The King Kasuals.

LATE 1963 Jimi journeys to New York via Philadelphia, where he plays some recording sessions – his first authenticated visit to a professional studio – with R&B performer Lonnie Youngblood.

EARLY 1964 In New York, Jimi joins The Isley Brothers' backing band, and begins to record and tour with them.

OCTOBER 1964 Jimi quits The Isleys' band and joins a touring group which supports musicians like Jackie Wilson and Sam Cooke.

DECEMBER 1964 Little Richard enlists Jimi for his touring band.

MARCH 1965 Jimi and future Love vocalist Arthur Lee collaborate on a single by Rose Lee Brooks.

JULY 1965 Little Richard fires Jimi for missing the bus after a New York show.

27 JULY 1965 Hendrix signs a two-year recording deal with R&B label Sue Records in New York.

OCTOBER 1965 In mid-town Manhattan, Jimi meets struggling R&B singer Curtis Knight, who invites him to join his band, The Squires.

15 OCTOBER 1965 Jimi signs another exclusive recording deal, this time with Curtis Knight's recording manager, Ed Chalpin of PPX Records. Knight and Hendrix record several studio and live sessions over the next few months.

JANUARY 1966 Leaving Curtis Knight, Jimi begins to perform with King Curtis's band.

MAY 1966 Jimi rejoins The Squires for two weeks of New York gigs, but leaves at the end of the first week. He plays briefly with Carl Holmes and The Commanders, before inaugurating his own band, The Rainflowers.

JUNE 1966 The Rainflowers become Jimmy James and The Blue Flames, with a line-up including future rock stars Randy California and Jeff 'Skunk' Baxter.

23 JUNE 1966 Keith Richards' girlfriend, Linda Keith, watches a Hendrix show in Manhattan, and tries to interest Stones manager Andrew Oldham in the group.

5 JULY 1966 As Oldham isn't impressed, Linda

Keith turns her attention to Animals' bassist Chas Chandler, who accompanies her to a Jimmy James & The Blue Flames performance at the Café Wah? in Greenwich Village.

9 SEPTEMBER 1966 After completing the final Animals tour, Chas revisits Jimi in New York, and offers to manage him and make him a star in England.

24 SEPTEMBER 1966 Jimi and Chas reach London: that night, Jimi plays in public for the first time in England.

29 SEPTEMBER 1966 Bassist Noel Redding is enlisted for Hendrix's new band: they begin rehearsals with drummer Aynsley Dunbar. Chas Chandler's business partner, Mike Jeffery, begins to take a keen interest in Hendrix's career.

5 OCTOBER 1966 Mitch Mitchell is appointed the permanent drummer in the band, now named The Jimi Hendrix Experience.

13 OCTOBER 1966 The Experience play their first gig, in Evreux near Paris.

23 OCTOBER 1966 Back in London, they record 'Hey Joe' with producer Chas Chandler and vocal support from The Breakaways.

2 NOVEMBER 1966 Jimi begins work on his début album.

13 DECEMBER 1966 The Experience make their TV début on ITV's *Ready, Steady, Go!*

30 JANUARY 1967 The Experience perform three songs at their début BBC Radio session.

3 FEBRUARY 1967 They start to record their second single, 'Purple Haze', and work on its follow-up, 'The Wind Cries Mary'.

31 MARCH 1967 The Experience begin a controversial UK tour supporting pop idols The Walker Brothers.

4 APRIL 1967 The final day of recording for the 'Are You Experienced' LP.

4 MAY 1967 Work begins at Olympic Studios on Jimi's second album.

18 JUNE 1967 The Experience play their first American concert, at the Monterey Pop Festival in California.

8 JULY 1967 In another mismatch, Hendrix and The Experience begin their first US tour, supporting the world's No. 1 teen idols, The Monkees.

16 JULY 1967 By mutual consent, the Experience play their final date on The Monkees' tour. Their publicists subsequently claim that their early departure is sparked by protests from The Daughters of the American Revolution.

30 JULY 1967 Jimi jams with former boss Curtis

Knight during a session at PPX Studios: the results of this reunion are later released by Ed Chalpin, prompting a flurry of lawsuits.

30 OCTOBER 1967 Work on 'Axis: Bold As Love', the second Experience album, is completed.

22 DECEMBER 1967 The Experience perform as part of the Christmas Pop Spectacular in London's Olympia Hall, on the same bill as The Who, Pink Floyd, Eric Burdon & The Animals, Soft Machine and The Move.

4 JANUARY 1968 Jimi is arrested in Gothenburg, Sweden, and charged with damaging his hotel room.

21 JANUARY 1968 He starts to record his version of Bob Dylan's 'All Along The Watchtower', the first track attempted for his third album.

25 FEBRUARY 1968 Jimi and the other Experience members – in both senses of the word – are immortalised in plaster by the Plaster Casters of Chicago.

13 MARCH 1968 At the Scene Club in New York, Jimi takes part in a drunken jam with Jim Morrison of The Doors.

18 APRIL 1968 Work begins in earnest at the Record Plant in New York on what becomes the 'Electric Ladyland' album.

18 MAY 1968 Hendrix interrupts his sessions to perform at the Miami Pop Festival.

27 AUGUST 1968 The final day of recording for 'Electric Ladyland'.

10 OCTOBER 1968 The Experience begin a short season of concerts at the Winterland Ballroom in San Francisco.

NOVEMBER 1968 Jimi produces an album for Cat Mother & The All Night Newsboys in New York.

4 JANUARY 1969 The Experience commemorate the break-up of Cream by performing an unplanned 'Sunshine Of Your Love' on the live TV programme, *The Lulu Show*, forcing the host to abandon her closing number.

14 FEBRUARY 1969 The Experience regroup at Olympic Studios in London to work abortively on a fourth album.

24 FEBRUARY 1969 A chaotic, often splendid show at the Royal Albert Hall in London is taped and filmed for future release.

MARCH 1969 Jimi produces several songs for an album by The Buddy Miles Express.

18 MARCH 1969 Jimi tapes a studio rendition of 'The Star Spangled Banner', which becomes a highlight of his subsequent live shows.

3 MAY 1969 Jimi is arrested for possession of illegal drugs on his arrival at Toronto International Airport.

29 JUNE 1969 A performance at the Denver Pop Festival becomes The Experience's final show when Noel Redding discovers that Hendrix is planning to replace him with Billy Cox.

10 JULY 1969 Jimi débuts his new band, with Mitch Mitchell and Billy Cox, on American TV's *The Tonight Show*.

14 AUGUST 1969 Jimi begins rehearsals with an extended line-up, adding a second guitarist, Larry Lee, plus percussionists Juma Sultan and Jerry Velez.

18 AUGUST 1969 The newly named Gypsy Sons & Rainbows Band headline the Woodstock festival in Bethel, New York.

28 AUGUST 1969 Jimi resumes work on another studio album, a year after completing 'Electric Ladyland'.

7 NOVEMBER 1969 After Mitch Mitchell returns to London to work on a solo project, Jimi enlists Billy Cox, Juma Sultan and drummer Buddy Miles to the Record Plant in New York, for sessions by what he comes to call The Band Of Gypsys.

10 DECEMBER 1969 Despite effectively admitting his guilt, Jimi is found not guilty of his drug possession charges in Toronto.

31 DECEMBER 1969 Jimi begins two nights of shows at the Fillmore East in New York, which are taped for the 'Band Of Gypsys' album – the rights to which are presented to Ed Chalpin in settlement of his outstanding contractual claim on Hendrix's services, dating back to 1965.

28 JANUARY 1970 Hendrix has to leave the stage after two songs of a New York performance with The Band Of Gypsys; the line-up is disbanded soon afterwards.

4 FEBRUARY 1970 Hendrix, Mitchell and Redding announce the reformation of The Jimi Hendrix Experience, though they never record or perform together again.

MARCH 1970 In London, Hendrix guests on sessions by Arthur Lee and Stephen Stills.

23 MARCH 1970 Mitch Mitchell and Billy Cox are established as Jimi's rhythm section for the first of a series of sessions, intended to spawn a double-album called 'The First Rays Of The New Rising Sun'.

30 MAY 1970 The trio – now known as the Cry Of Love band – are taped and filmed during their performance at the Berkeley Community Theater in California.

15 JUNE 1970 Jimi inaugurates his own Electric

Lady Studios in New York, though they aren't officially opened for another two months.

30 JULY 1970 The Cry Of Love band perform two shows on the Hawaiian island of Maui, which are filmed for a documentary movie eventually released as Rainbow Bridge.

1 AUGUST 1970 Jimi performs his last US concert.

22 AUGUST 1970 Jimi's final recording session takes place at Electric Lady Studios, as he tapes his solo rendition of 'Belly Button Window'.

26 AUGUST 1970 The Electric Lady studio complex is officially opened.

27 AUGUST 1970 Hendrix flies to England.

30 AUGUST 1970 Jimi, Mitch and Billy perform an erratic show at the Isle Of Wight festival in England.

2 SEPTEMBER 1970 Three songs into his performance in Aarhus, Denmark, Jimi has to leave the stage, suffering from too heavy a dose of sleeping pills.

6 SEPTEMBER 1970 At the Fehmarn festival in Germany, Hendrix's last full live performance is greeted with sporadic booing by an ill-tempered crowd. Jimi then flies to London.

10 SEPTEMBER 1970 Journalist Keith Altham conducts Jimi's last interview.

16/17 SEPTEMBER 1970 Jimi makes his last appearance on stage at Ronnie Scott's club in London, jamming with Eric Burdon and War.

18 SEPTEMBER 1970 Ambulances are called to the Samarkand Hotel in London, where Jimi is found unconscious, having vomited in his sleep. The ambulance-men are unable to revive him. He is taken to St. Mary Abbot's Hospital, where he is officially pronounced dead just after midday.

28 SEPTEMBER 1970 At a London inquest, the coroner instructs the jury to return an open verdict on Hendrix's death, which is blamed on "inhalation of vomit due to barbiturate intoxication".

1 OCTOBER 1970 James Marshall Hendrix is buried in Greenwood Cemetery, Renton, Seattle.

THE CAST-LIST

JIMI HENDRIX Born Johnny Allen Hendrix, 27th November 1942, Seattle. Died 18th September 1970, London

ED CHALPIN Producer of Hendrix's sessions with Curtis Knight for Chalpin's own PPX label. Jimi signed an exclusive recording deal with Chalpin, and never cancelled it.

CHAS CHANDLER Former bassist with The Animals, who 'discovered' Hendrix playing in the New York clubs. With his partner, Mike Jeffery, Chandler masterminded Jimi's commercial breakthrough. Chas took particular interest in the music, producing the first two Experience albums.

BILLY COX Ex-Army buddy of Hendrix, who was recruited to play in all Jimi's touring groups from the summer of 1969 until his death.

ALAN DOUGLAS Record producer, label owner and associate of Hendrix from 1969 until the end of Jimi's life. Douglas was left in possession of several Hendrix tapes, and subsequently became involved in assembling posthumous releases. Since 1980, he has ostensibly controlled the Hendrix Estate's handling of Jimi's musical catalogue.

MIKE JEFFERY Co-manager of Hendrix from 1966 onwards with Chas Chandler, taking sole command after Chandler retired from the fray in 1969. After Jimi's death, he oversaw the release of the initial posthumous albums, until he was killed in a 1973 plane crash.

CURTIS KNIGHT Struggling soul singer in 1965, who recruited Hendrix as guitarist with his band, The Squires. He recorded with Jimi in 1965 and again in the summer of 1967, and has written two books about their relationship.

EDDIE KRAMER Studio engineer from England, who became one of America's leading producer/engineers. He worked with Hendrix from late 1966 until his death, and also contributed his skills to many of the posthumous releases.

BUDDY MILES Former drummer with The

Electric Flag and The Buddy Miles Express, who worked with Hendrix intermittently in 1968, and then formed the Band Of Gypsys with him in late 1969, until early 1970.

MITCH MITCHELL Teenage drumming prodigy, who was recruited for The Jimi Hendrix Experience in 1966, and remained with Jimi – except for the Band Of Gypsys – until his death.

NOEL REDDING The bassist in The Jimi Hendrix Experience, who departed in the summer of 1969 to concentrate on his own spin-off band, Fat Mattress. Also contributed occasional songs/vocals to Experience albums.

JUMA SULTAN Percussionist who first joined Hendrix's band just before Woodstock, and worked with him intermittently in the studio and on stage for the next year.

LONNIE YOUNGBLOOD Like Curtis Knight, an otherwise forgotten R&B artist, who sang and played sax on some 1963 recordings which featured Hendrix on tentative guitar. Without Youngblood's blessing, scores of albums have been released featuring his Sixties work with Jimi, many of them 'faked' by adding a Hendrix imitator to existing Jimi-less tracks.

THE ORIGINAL ALBUMS

During his lifetime, Jimi Hendrix approved the release of just four albums, and tacitly condoned another. Only one was conceived and achieved to his total satisfaction – total, that is, apart from the cover artwork, which he deplored.

'Are You Experienced' and 'Axis: Bold As Love' were both completed in 1967, with creative control shared by Hendrix and his manager/producer, Chas Chandler. The two records were assembled with a haste typical of the period: only The Beatles, and to a lesser extent The Rolling Stones, had been allowed carte blanche in the studio to work at their own pace.

When Hendrix and Chandler parted company, early in the creation of 'Electric Ladyland', Jimi assumed total command. The album was begun in December 1967, and not completed until August 1968, by which time Jimi had recorded enough raw material to fill several double albums.

And that, remarkably, was the final studio LP of Jimi Hendrix's career. Between August 1968 and his death in September 1970, Jimi completed work on just one single – and that was pulled from the shops within days of release, when he suddenly lost faith in its artistic credentials. Two more LPs were released under his name, but both of them were blatant compromises – 'Smash Hits' being intended as an obvious stopgap, 'Band Of Gypsys' as a deliberately ineffectual piece of contractual obligation.

When Jimi died, his next studio record, provisionally entitled 'The First Rays Of The New Rising Sun', was long overdue. Several dozen tracks were in various stages of completion, but none of them was actually mixed and mastered. It was left to drummer Mitch Mitchell and engineer Eddie Kramer to assemble 'The Cry Of Love', the first of a long series of outside attempts to read the mind of an artist who had patently lost confidence in his own judgement.

During the decades that followed, 'Are You

experienced', 'Axis. Bold As Love' and 'Electric Ladyland' were regarded as sacrosanct by those who appointed themselves as Jimi's artistic executors. There was a minor problem with 'Are You Experienced', which had been issued in different forms in Britain and America, but no-one dared to tamper with Jimi's original vision of his early studio catalogue.

These strict guidelines were maintained until 1993, when Alan Douglas – self-selected as the keeper of the Hendrix flame, and effective controller of Jimi's musical legacy for the best part of 20 years – called a press conference at the opening of his Jimi Hendrix Exhibition at the Ambassador Gallery in New York. He used the occasion to announce that the increasingly lucrative Hendrix musical estate was being moved from US Warner Brothers, who'd been controlling the American release schedule since Jimi's death, to MCA. At the same time, he revealed that he had set in motion plans to update the three 'classic' Hendrix albums – to dress them in clothes more appropriate to the dawn of the 21st century.

"Everything in the present catalogue is a budget release," he explained, "and every-thing's got skimpy packaging. They're all 25-year-old packages. I want to take high-level, contemporary graphic art, put it on the covers and use the old jackets on the back. I don't want people to think it's a new record: they should know it's a reissue of the original record, with all these new elements that we're incorporating into it."

Questioned about his rights to tamper with Jimi's work, Douglas responded tartly: "Jimi Hendrix is not here. He put it into my hands." Fans were quick to disagree with Douglas's assertions, but within a few weeks the new packages were in the shops – bearing artwork that was undeniably stylish but completely out of keeping with the original designs. Critics slammed Douglas for the many typos and inaccuracies on the sets; the curator replied that he'd been forced into delivering the packages too quickly, and that the mistakes would be corrected as soon as the initial supplies were exhausted. In retrospect, it was a battle over nothing: the result of Douglas's intervention is that Hendrix's three studio masterpieces are currently available on CD in their best ever sound quality, with packaging and annotation to match. That's much more than you could boast for, as an example, The Rolling Stones

ARE YOU EXPERIENCED?

The three original Experience albums are perfect encapsulations of their eras. While 'Axis: Bold As Love' testifies to Jimi's increasing musical sophistication and 'Electric Ladyland' to his boundless artistic vision, 'Are You Experienced' (produced by Chas Chandler) looks both backwards, to his years as an R&B guitarist, and forwards to the sonic discoveries to come. Its wide variety of styles and rhythms means that it lacks the internal unity of his later work, but it is still – particularly in its current enlarged form on CD – the perfect introduction to his music.

ARE YOU EXPERIENCED?

(VERSION 1)

LP RELEASE: TRACK 613 001 (UK), MAY 1967

CD RELEASE: POLYDOR 825 416-2 (GERMANY),

APRIL 1985

Tracks: Foxy Lady/Manic Depression/ Red House/Can You See Me/Love Or Confusion/I Don't Live Today/May This Be Love/Fire/Third Stone From The Sun/ Remember/Are You Experienced

This is the original UK track listing of the album, as prepared by Hendrix and Chas Chandler in 1967, shoved on to CD in the mid-Eighties with the bare minimum of thought. There's no evidence of digital remastering on this package, but plenty of annoying hiss and distortion. Typical of the thoughtless slap-it-out mentality is the retention of the original 1967 sleeve-notes, with their erroneous assertion that Jimi was born in 1947.

Note that the version of 'Can You See Me' on this disc, manufactured in Germany for the entire UK and European market, is slightly different from the original LP cut.

ARE YOU EXPERIENCED?

(VERSION 2)

LP RELEASE: REPRISE RS 6261 (USA),
AUGUST 1967

CD RELEASE: REPRISE 6261-2 (USA)

Tracks: Purple Haze/Manic Depression/Hey Joe/Love Or Confusion/May This Be Love/I Don't Live Today/The Wind Cries Mary/Fire/Third Stone From The Sun/Foxy Lady/Are You Experienced?

The original American release of 'Experienced' neatly omitted the album's two weakest tracks, 'Remember' and 'Can You See Me', in favour of the A-sides of Jimi's first three singles. But 'Red House' was also sacrificed, with the result that US audiences were denied evidence of Jimi's vital blues roots.

The first pressing of the American CD suffered from the same sonic flaws as its UK equivalent. It was subsequently remastered in mid-1989, and reissued with 'RE-1' etched into the centre of the disc (as were 'Axis' and 'Electric Ladyland').

ARE YOU EXPERIENCED?

(VERSION 3)

POLYDOR 847 234-2 (GERMANY), JUNE 1991

Tracks: as Version 2

When 'Are You Experienced' was at last remastered with some degree of care for the 'Sessions' boxed set, the involvement of Alan Douglas's US team of engineers meant that it was the American issue of the album that was corrected – therefore becoming the standard, albeit briefly, for the entire world.

ARE YOU EXPERIENCED?

(VERSION 4)

POLYDOR 521 036-2 (GERMANY), OCTOBER 1993

Tracks: Hey Joe/Stone Free/Purple Haze/51st Anniversary/The Wind Cries Mary/Highway Chile/Foxy Lady/Manic Depression/Red House/Can You See Me/Love Or Confusion/I Don't Live Today/May This Be Love/Fire/Third Stone From The Sun/Remember/Are You Experienced

At last, a new standard for a new age: an entirely remastered and repackaged album, with generic artwork utilising period photos by Gered Mankowitz, brilliantly transformed by the Wherefore Art? design team. The pathetic

4-page inserts of previous CDs are replaced by a de luxe 24-page affair, stuffed full of informative, if sometimes pretentious, notes by Michael Fairchild. (The reverse of the CD package explains helpfully that the album "is a key to the union of ancient and futuristic urges".) On the back cover of the booklet, alongside a sheet of detachable Experience adhesive stamps, is a reproduction of the original front cover artwork, for the purists amongst us. (The same approach was utilised for revamps of the Axis: Bold As Love and Electric Ladyland CDs.)

The track listing has also been reworked, with the intention of combining the UK and US contents, plus relevant bonus cuts. To preserve the chronological sequence, the A- and B-sides of The Experience's first three singles have been added to the start of the album, before the entire original track listing follows.

Just one exception to this rule, though: the version of 'Red House' on this CD is not the one that Hendrix and Chandler approved back in '67. It's actually a fatter, but somehow less exhilarating alternate take, originally released on the American Smash Hits LP. Or,

as Fairchild puts it, "Jimi's vocal is more developed while his guitar lines build flawlessly to a synaptic climax." Nevertheless, its appearance here countermands Hendrix's original instructions, and is the only serious flaw with this reissue package.

TRACK-BY-TRACK:

HEY JOE

The song chosen as the A-side of Hendrix's first single had a complex history. It was written by Californian folksinger Billy Roberts, who needed a quick buck and sold it to Dino Valenti, leader of the Quicksilver Messenger Service. Valenti copyrighted it under the pen-name Chet Powers, and taught the song to his Greenwich Village friend, David Crosby. With The Byrds, Crosby began to perform a frantic arrangement of the song in 1965, but before they could record it, they were beaten by fellow LA band The Leaves.

After all that, it was folkie Tim Rose who concocted the slow, bluesy arrangement which, in turn, Hendrix learned in 1966. It became the first song The Experience ever recorded, on October 23 that year, aided by the backing vocals of session singers The Breakaways.

STONE FREE

"Jimi wanted to put 'Land Of 1000 Dances' on the B-side," recalled Chas Chandler, "but I said no way – you will sit down tonight and write a new song." 'Stone Free', a swaggering, hipspeaking piece of rock funk, was the result of this October 24 writing session. Its vibrant rhythmic pulse is camouflaged on CD by the paper-thin reproduction. Jimi revamped the song in April 1969, as partially documented on Crash Landing.

PURPLE HAZE

From its ominously out-of-step guitar intro to its howling whammy-bar finale, 'Purple Haze' captured all the threatening adventurism of the early Experience. You could break down the influences, from Stax R&B to The Beatles' Revolver, but nothing on earth sounded like 'Purple Haze' in January 1967, when the basic ingredients of this track were cut.

51ST ANNIVERSARY

A close musical cousin of the album track 'Can You See Me', '51st Anniversary' is perhaps the most unlikely lyrical concept in the entire Hendrix catalogue – dominated as it is by fantasies of sexual bravado, romance, and excursions into mind and space. '51st Anniversary' tackled the more prosaic subject of marriage, and its potential drawbacks – apparently inspired by the collapse of his parents' union many years earlier.

THE WIND CRIES MARY

On the same day as 'Purple Haze', the Experience taped this poignant love song, dedicated to Jimi's girlfriend of the time, Kathy Mary Etchingham. Producer Chas Chandler recollects that it took twenty minutes to record, from Jimi's first performance of the song to the band to the final guitar overdub.

HIGHWAY CHILE

Cut at the same April 3, 1967, session as the magnificent 'Are You Experienced', 'Highway Chile' was a relatively lacklustre, if enjoyably unpretentious, piece of rock-blues. It borrowed a guitar figure from the fade of 'Purple Haze', and generally exhibited all the traits of a song composed to order rather than inspiration.

FOXY LADY

The original 'Are You Experienced' album opened with this feast of sexual innuendo and guitar distortion, set to a slowed version of Wilson Pickett's Memphis soul beat. The first few seconds of vibrato wound up a tension that the rest of the LP rarely let lapse. 'Foxy Lady' was one of the first songs cut for the album, in December 1966.

MANIC DEPRESSION

An epic of confusion and slightly amused despair, 'Manic Depression' set Jimi's spiralling guitar against the cascading drum fills of Mitch Mitchell. The lyrics caught Jimi between emotional poles, unable to achieve any more coherent response to his world than "It's a frustrating mess". But the guitar solo expressed the point of the song more eloquently, nearly tumbling out of time before Hendrix steered it back into the verse. The track was begun in February 1967 and completed in March.

RED HOUSE

On March 29, 1967, The Experience taped several versions of this Fifties-style slow blues. One version, sometimes little more than a tentative jam, but with a sense of discovery that made it irresistible, ended up on the British release of the LP. On CD, that's now been replaced by a more confident but less magical take, with more pronounced vocal echo. They're both superb, but for authenticity's sake, I wish the earlier take was on the CD.

CAN YOU SEE ME

'Can You See Me', taped on November 2, 1966, was a contender for the flipside of 'Hey Joe'. Instead, its updated blues theme, built around a nagging guitar riff, ended up on 'Are You Experienced'. There was an air of novelty about the entire performance, from its double-tracked vocals to the guitar pulsing from speaker to speaker, but it was undeniably exciting.

LOVE OR CONFUSION

Magical and dark, 'Love Or Confusion' was in a different league to 'Can You See Me'. Its eerie vocal echo and droning guitar suggested that the second of the two alternatives in the title was closer to the mark. The song dated from the earliest Experience sessions, and was then completed in April 1967.

I DON'T LIVE TODAY

On February 20, 1967, The Jimi Hendrix Experience stretched rock into new territory with this magnificently malevolent psychic voyage. Even without the grim fatalism of the lyrics, the music alone would be enough to chart the shift from despair through death into some strange kind of reincarnation, as sirens, dive bombs and animal cries punctuate the tribal ritual of Mitch Mitchell's drums.

MAY THIS BE LOVE

Behind almost every song on 'Are You Experienced', Mitch Mitchell unfurled hypnotic, unsettling drum rhythms – even when the material was as gentle and romantic as this song from early April 1967. Besides the beauty of Hendrix's melody, check the sonic painting of his opening guitar figures, and spaciness of Chas Chandler's production.

FIRE

Inspired by an inconsequential incident at Noel Redding's house, 'Fire' returned Hendrix to the R&B circuit, on a song that would have sounded equally at home on an Otis Redding album. Once again, Mitch Mitchell had a field day during the session.

THIRD STONE FROM THE SUN

Musical science-fiction became a mini-genre in Hendrix's work with The Experience, pioneered by this instrumental from April 1967. Its riff – later borrowed by Cozy Powell for his hit, 'Dance With The Devil' – was a throwback to the early 60s era of surf guitar band; hence the ironic reference during the track's slowed-down dialogue sequence, to the fact that "you need never hear surf music again". That dialogue proved to be between space commanders, approaching the planet from afar; 'Third Stone' also offered some intergalactic poetry, and a couple of minutes of tomfoolery on the control-room faders.

REMEMBER

Like 'Fire', this mid-pace song, recorded on

February 8, 1967, was proof that Jimi had spent a couple of years on the American R&B circuit. Even the imagery, with its use of soul staples like "mockingbirds", sounded second-hand. Amazing guitar solo, though.

ARE YOU EXPERIENCED?

Wiper-blades of backwards tape; drum rhythms from some perverted tattoo; guitars that howled like wounded saxophones; and a voice of blank resignation – these were the constituent parts of a song that begged the answer 'yes', but hinted that the psychedelic journey might not lead the traveller into the light. 'Are You Experienced?' was the strongest track on the album, a four-minute display of all Hendrix's angst and skill in April 1967.

AXIS: BOLD AS LOVE

Within seven months of 'Are You Experienced', 'Axis: Bold As Love' heralded a new subtlety in Hendrix's work — and a clear mingling of black and white musical inspirations. The début album showed what happened when an R&B musician discovered psychedelic rock; this follow-up made the journey in reverse. Cut almost entirely in the last week of October 1967, with Chas Chandler once again as producer, it was a more unified effort than 'Experienced', but still wavered in mood from electronic experimentation to lyrical balladry, via one overt exercise in political intervention.

AXIS: BOLD AS LOVE

LP RELEASE: TRACK 613 003 (UK), DECEMBER 1967
CD RELEASE: POLYDOR 813 572-2 (GERMANY), 1987
Tracks: EXP/Up From The Skies/Spanish Castle Magic/Wait Until Tomorrow/Ain't No Telling/Little Wing/If Six Was Nine/You've Got Me Floating/Castles Made Of Sand/She's So Fine/One Rainy Wish/Little Miss Lover/Bold As Love
Like the rest of the initial batch of Polydor CDs, this release did more to damn the new medium rather than recommend it – thanks to some hamfisted editing, dubious mastering, and almost total lack of annotation.

AXIS: BOLD AS LOVE
(VERSION 2)
REISSUED AS POLYDOR 847-243-2 (GERMANY), JUNE 1991
Tracks: as above
Sonically improved, but still not perfect (note the hiss on 'Up From The Skies', as an example), this was the version of the 'Axis' CD found in the Sessions box set.

AXIS: BOLD AS LOVE
(VERSION 3)
POLYDOR 847-243-2 (GERMANY), LATE 1993
Tracks: as above
The 'official' remastering job on 'Axis' was

every bit as triumphant as the revamped 'Are You Experienced', although this time Alan Douglas didn't add any bonus tracks. Like its companion CDs, this album had its original cover sentenced to the back of the package, while a computer-enhanced Gered Mankowitz photograph fronted the booklet — which had detailed notes by Michael Fairchild.

TRACK-BY-TRACK:

EXP

'Symphony Of Experience' was the working title of this tongue-in-cheek representation of the arrival of a creature from outer space – introduced by Mitch Mitchell of "Radio EXP" as "Paul Caruso", who was an American friend of Jimi's. Hendrix's voice supplied the role of Caruso, followed by an exemplary barrage of guitar effects.

UP FROM THE SKIES

After the sonic assault of 'EXP', the brushed-drums, restrained wah-wah and gentle jazz rhythms of 'Up From The Skies' marked the first of a series of profound switches of mood and tempo on 'Axis: Bold As Love'. Having

unveiled his full palette of space noises, our galactic visitor literally came down to earth, to the dark recognition of "the smell of a world that has burned".

SPANISH CASTLE MAGIC

In his late teens, Jimi and his friends used to hang out at the Spanish Castle, a jazz club a few miles out of the Seattle city limits. Almost a decade later, he celebrated its attractions in song – though the lyrical inspiration ("It's all in your mind", he sang at one point) mattered less than the sheer effervescence of Jimi's performance, repeated again and again over the next three years as 'Spanish Castle Magic' became a staple in his live sets.

WAIT UNTIL TOMORROW

If you crossed 'Stone Free' with 'Fire', this would be the result – a cool, laidback but still concerned piece of romantic role-playing, wrapped around a sinuous guitar-line, and supported by some white-boy soul vocals from Messrs. Redding and Mitchell.

AIN'T NO TELLING

Like 'Wait Until Tomorrow', 'Ain't No Telling' had its roots in R&B, and Jimi's experiences in road-bands from 1964 to 1966. It was hinged around a call-and-response vocal lick, which ignited into a slyly simple guitar solo.

LITTLE WING

If much of the 'Axis' album was inspired by Atlantic and Stax R&B, there were several hints that Jimi had been listening closely to the melodic guitar-playing of The Impressions' frontman, Curtis Mayfield. The wonderfully lyrical solo which opens the song started with a punctuation mark, and then prepared the listener for the exquisite verbal imagery to follow. Between verses, Mitch Mitchell added some superb drum fills, while the delicacy of the production was perfected by Jimi's one-note-to-the-bar glockenspiel, which supported the emotional fragility of the piece.

IF SIX WAS NINE

In stark contrast, 'If Six Was Nine' carried the album's starkest sound, as the guitar riff and drums combined to create a martial atmos-phere. There was no conscious smoothing of the production on this confrontational song, with its free-form guitar solo and equally forceful contribution from Mitchell backing up the radicalism and pride of the lyrics. Recorded in May 1967, five months before most of the LP, 'If Six Was Nine' prefigured the politicised funk anthems of Sly Stone in 1969.

YOU'VE GOT ME FLOATING

Back to the bars: 'You've Got Me Floating' was formulaic R&B, in the tradition of 'Ain't No Telling', with only the cross-speaker fades to pull it into the psychedelic age.

CASTLES MADE OF SAND

The second of Jimi's Mayfield-inspired guitar intros led into a regretful tale of fractured dreams. Some of his most beautiful lyrical imagery explored the failure of a marriage (probably his parents', as on '51st Anniversary'), the realisation of his own artistic limitations, and then in a clever reversal of his theme, the birth of hope from the brink of utter despair. Hendrix never sounded more vulnerable, or closer to the spirit of a song.

SHE'S SO FINE

Time for another abrupt change of mood, via Noel Redding's début as a composer and lead vocalist. His lyrics owed much to the dislocation of British psychedelic pop, from 'Revolver' to Pink Floyd, while the music soared from Hendrix-flavoured soul to a blatant tribute to The Who in the middle eight – echoed by Jimi's Townshend-like guitar solo.

ONE RAINY WISH

Jimi's close study of The Impressions' catalogue inspired another melodic guitar prelude for a suitably misty dream-vision. More than 'Little Wing' or 'Castles Made Of Sand', 'One Rainy Wish' seemed to owe something to chemical stimulation, which would explain the inexact, yet highly colourful, dreamscape Jimi unveiled. Twin guitars cascaded minute variations on a guitar riff, to bring the song to a close.

LITTLE MISS LOVER

From dream to sexual desire, as Jimi revived the lusty spirit of Don Covay or Wilson Pickett's R&B with a guitar riff that would have delighted James Brown. So would

Mitch's drum intro, which cleverly set the pattern for what Jimi played through the rest of the song.

BOLD AS LOVE

The mystery of the album title was explained in its final song: as Jimi sang, "just ask the axis". That might have been "the axis of the earth", as he claimed in one interview, or some more nebulous spiritual concept; or simply a prettier way of ending each chorus than saying: "You better believe it".

Treading a lyrical tightrope with spectacular skill, Jimi unwound a lengthy personal metaphor with a series of colour images, and then collected the fragments of his soul in the title phrase. After two verses, he decided he could speak more eloquently with his guitar, setting out on a liberating one-minute solo that faded away, then (in what Jimi called elsewhere a 'slight return') regrouped with renewed energy to restate the melodic theme of the song. It was a typically subtle climax to an album which divided itself between R&B dramatics and near-confessional poetry.

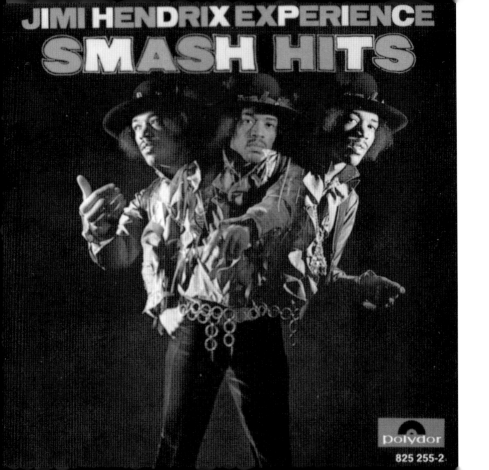

SMASH HITS

SMASH HITS
(VERSION 1)
LP RELEASE: TRACK 613 004 (UK), APRIL 1968
CD RELEASE: POLYDOR 825 255-2 (UK), FEBRUARY 1985

Tracks: Purple Haze/Fire/The Wind Cries Mary/Can You See Me/51st Anniversary/Hey Joe/Stone Free/The Stars That Play With Laughing Sam's Dice/Manic Depression/Highway Chile/The Burning Of The Midnight Lamp/Foxy Lady

THE ALBUM: During what was, for the 1960s, a lengthy pause between the release of 'Axis: Bold As Love' at the end of 1967 and 'Electric Ladyland' almost a year later, Track Records in London grew perturbed by the suggestion that the record-buying public might forget who Jimi Hendrix was. To maintain his profile, they hastily assembled 'Smash Hits', with its stunning triple-exposure cover almost overshadowed by the crass, comic-style lettering. Nothing on the album was new, but the album did at least collect together Jimi's pre-1968 non-album singles.

THE CD: In the first stirrings of the CD era, Polydor were quite happy to tumble fifth-generation tapes onto a disgustingly poor compact disc transfer. It's hard to know where the criticisms should begin: choose for yourselves between the back cover and booklet shot of Jimi apparently playing guitar right-handed, the atrocious sound quality (check the almost unlistenable reproduction of the stoned mayhem of 'Stars That Play With Laughing Sam's Dice') or the fact that the CD clips the first half-second off at least three tracks, 'Fire', 'The Wind Cries Mary' and 'Stone Free'. Listening to the finished disc with any consideration of quality control was obviously beyond Polydor's engineers.

Ten of these twelve tracks are now available in far superior quality on the revamped 'Are You Experienced?', while 'Burning Of The Midnight Lamp' is best heard on 'Electric Ladyland'. The last possible reason for owning this CD dissolves when you discover that 'Stars That Play With Laughing Sam's Dice' was included in much more impressive quality, and in stereo not mono, on the otherwise dismal 'Loose Ends' CD. As it stands, this release is the worst CD in the 'official' catalogue.

SMASH HITS
(VERSION 2)
LP RELEASE: REPRISE MS 2025 (USA), JULY 1969
CD RELEASE: REPRISE 2776-2 (USA)

Tracks: Purple Haze/Fire/The Wind Cries Mary/Can You See Me/Hey Joe/Stone Free/Manic Depression/Foxy Lady/Crosstown Traffic/All Along The Watchtower/Red House/Remember/51st Anniversary/ Highway Chile

America missed out on the first transfer of 'Smash Hits' to CD, for which they should be grateful. By 1989, digital remastering made this set a much more attractive option than its UK counterpart – especially for those with CD Video players, as the Hendrix Estate's engineers had added video graphics to the delights of the music.

The track listing of this set added '51st Anniversary' and 'Highway Chile' to the original US line-up of the LP – though not 'Stars

That Play With Laughing Sam's Dice', which never appeared in America during Jimi's lifetime. Its inclusion on this CD would have neatly collected all the original Experience A- and B-sides on one package.

823 359-2 [MH2]

Polydor

THE JIMI HENDRIX EXPERIENCE
ELECTRIC LADYLAND

ELECTRIC LADYLAND

For pure experimental genius, melodic flair, conceptual vision and instrumental brilliance, 'Electric Ladyland' is a prime contender for the status of rock's greatest album. During its 75-minute passage, it flirts with electronic composition, soft-soul, delta blues, psychedelic rock, modern jazz, and proto-funk, without ever threatening to be confined by any of those labels. It climaxed with a display of musical virtuosity that has never been surpassed in rock music. Small wonder that Hendrix found the task of matching this album insuperable: despite the splendour of much of his post-1968 work, he could never again capture the effortless magic of 'Electric Ladyland'.

The album was a landmark in personal terms as much as artistic. During the early sessions, Chas Chandler effectively resigned as Hendrix's producer; his formal disengagement as co-manager followed the next year. Meanwhile, internal dissension within The Jimi Hendrix Experience led Noel Redding to be absent for many of the 'Ladyland' sessions. Sometimes Hendrix covered his parts himself; sometimes he augmented his three-man studio line-up to incorporate keyboards, brass or woodwinds.

Most importantly, Jimi was able to expand the visionary painting-in-sound techniques he'd employed on tracks like 'Third Stone From The Sun' and 'EXP', to the point that he was able to build an entire side of the original double-LP – from 'Rainy Day, Dream Away' to 'Moon, Turn The Tides' – into an exotic suite, a seamless composition of fragments and improvisation that couldn't quite be categorised as jazz or as rock. Fracturing those genre boundaries merely made it more difficult for Jimi to reconstitute them in the future.

ELECTRIC LADYLAND

(VERSION 1)

LP RELEASE: TRACK 613 008/009 (UK), OCTOBER 1968

CD RELEASE: POLYDOR 823 359-2 (UK),

NOVEMBER 1984

Tracks:

CD1: ...And The Gods Made Love/Have You Ever Been (To Electric Ladyland)/ Crosstown Traffic/Voodoo Chile/Still Raining, Still Dreaming/House Burning Down/All Along The Watchtower/Voodoo Child (Slight Return)

CD2: Little Miss Strange/Long Hot Summer Night/Come On (Part 1)/Gypsy Eyes/The Burning Of The Midnight Lamp/Rainy Day, Dream Away/1983... (A Merman I Should Turn To Be)/Moon, Turn The Tides... Gently Gently Away

The original CD release retained the naked 'glory' of the original album cover, with its parade of slightly distorted female flesh. Hendrix hated that design, and he would have loathed these CDs even more. Not only was the mastering very poor, bathed in hiss and excess noise, but Polydor destroyed the original album concept by combining sides 1 and 4 of the double-LP on the first disc, and 2 and 3 on the second. This magnificent piece of logic meant that 'Rainy Day, Dream Away' appeared after its intended sequel, 'Still Raining, Still Dreaming'.

ELECTRIC LADYLAND

(VERSION 2)

POLYDOR 847 233-2 (GERMANY), JUNE 1991

Tracks: ...And The Gods Made Love/Have You Ever Been (To Electric Ladyland)/ Crosstown Traffic/Voodoo Chile/Little Miss Strange/Long Hot Summer Night/Come On (Part 1)/Gypsy Eyes/The Burning Of The Midnight Lamp/Rainy Day, Dream Away/ 1983 ...(A Merman I Should Turn To Be)/ Moon, Turn The Tides... Gently Gently Away/ Still Raining, Still Dreaming/House Burning Down/All Along The Watchtower/Voodoo Child (Slight Return)

During the initial phase of remastering for the 'Sessions' box set, 'Electric Ladyland' was sensibly reduced to a single CD (without shedding any of its contents), and the running-order was restored to Hendrix's original instructions. But the sound quality was only marginally more satisfactory than the first release.

ELECTRIC LADYLAND
(VERSION 3)
POLYDOR 847 233-2 (GERMANY), LATE 1993

Tracks: as Version 2

Excellently re-mastered, 'Electric Ladyland' now sounds as breath-taking on CD as it did on vinyl in 1968. Michael Fairchild's notes in the lengthy booklet are superb, and so is the sound quality – from the tumultuous sonic landslide of 'Voodoo Child (Slight Return)' to the delicacy of 'Moon, Turn The Tides' – which, bizarrely, is listed on the back cover as lasting for just one minute, not ten.

TRACK-BY-TRACK:

...AND THE GODS MADE LOVE

Originally conceived under the more prosaic title 'At Last The Beginning', this solo guitar concoction presaged the multi-dubbed delights to come, as Hendrix conjured magnificent pictures from musical genius and technical brilliance. Taped on June 29, 1968, during a single lengthy session.

HAVE YOU EVER BEEN (TO ELECTRIC LADYLAND)

Unlike the slightly later solo rendition captured on the 'Loose Ends' album, this soft-soul classic added studio trickery to the obvious influence of Curtis Mayfield's guitar. With Noel absent from the proceedings, Jimi handled the bass as well, and topped off a delightfully airy confection with some precise falsetto vocals.

CROSSTOWN TRAFFIC

Having just exhibited his command of the most subtle forms of soul music, Hendrix unveiled an aggressive, swaggering funk track – the basic track cut live in the studio by the Experience line-up back in December 1967, and then overdubbed in April and May 1968. Twenty-two years later, the Estate sanctioned the creation of a video to accompany the song's belated release as a single: both visually and aurally, it felt stunningly contemporary alongside the funk/rock crossovers of Lenny Kravitz and Living Colour.

Proof that someone at the sessions had a sense of humour was the involvement of

Traffic guitarist Dave Mason – whose sole contribution to the track was to sing the name of his band in every chorus.

VOODOO CHILE

Throughout 1967, Muddy Waters' Chicago R&B song, 'Catfish Blues', was a regular inclusion in the Experience's live set. By early 1968, it had mutated into an original Hendrix song, built around an identical riff, and with lyrics that paid their dues to some of the most unsettling images from the delta blues tradition.

During a lengthy session on May 1, 1968, Hendrix, Mitch Mitchell, Jack Casady (from Jefferson Airplane) and Steve Winwood (from Traffic) worked their way through a series of lengthy free-form jams around the 'Voodoo Chile' changes. This was the longest, and most successful, with Hendrix's surprisingly orthodox blues playing acting as counterpoint to Winwood's sustained organ chords.

Down the years, there's been much confusion over the exact spelling of this song, and its counterpart at the end of this album. I've settled on 'Voodoo Chile', but 'Voodoo Child (Slight Return)', as being Hendrix's preferences. What matters most, though, is that the two songs – offering vastly different takes on the blues – are the twin pillars of 'Electric Ladyland'.

LITTLE MISS STRANGE

For the second album running, Noel Redding was allowed to contribute – and sing – one number. Sadly, 'Little Miss Strange' did little more than repeat the ingredients of 'She's So Fine' from 'Axis', and 'Electric Ladyland' would be a stronger album without it. Like much of this set, it was taped during April and May 1968.

LONG HOT SUMMER NIGHT

Hendrix doubled up on bass and guitar, while Al Kooper's keyboards took a minor role on this piece of urban soul, which was mixed idiosyncratically, to say the least. Mitch Mitchell's drums were marooned on the far left of the stereo picture, while the other instruments never quite cohered into any kind of whole – as if the tape had picked up musicians from different rooms who happened by chance to be performing the same number.

COME ON (PART 1)

The final song to be recorded for the album was this cover of a blues by New Orleans guitarist Earl King, cut on August 27, 1968. The Experience ploughed through the standard chord changes and lyrical imagery, take after take, and several near-identical versions have appeared on bootlegs in recent years. Pleasant but undemanding, its last-minute addition to the album was strange, in view of the fact that Jimi left out-takes from these sessions like 'South Saturn Delta' and 'My Friend' unreleased.

GYPSY EYES

From its train-in-tunnel drum phrasing to its staccato guitar licks, 'Gypsy Eyes' was a masterpiece of creating substance out of little more than a riff and a message of love. Hendrix's guitar patterns on this track, and the interplay he built up with his own bass runs, can be heard resounding down the history of subsequent rock/funk crossovers, notably Prince's early-to-mid Eighties work.

THE BURNING OF THE MIDNIGHT LAMP

Already issued as a single long before the release of Electric Ladyland, 'Midnight Lamp' still fitted the album with its dense production (reminiscent of Phil Spector), unusual voicings (Jimi on harpsichord and mellotron) and evocative imagery. "They said that was the worst record we'd done," Jimi said in 1968, "but to me that was the best one we ever made."

RAINY DAY, DREAM AWAY

On June 10, 1968, Hendrix, Buddy Miles, organist Michael Finnigan, sax player Freddie Smith and percussionist Larry Faucette jammed through a set of jazzy changes with a cool, late-night feel, and an equally laidback lyric. Suitably overdubbed and edited, their lengthy 'Rainy Day Jam' was divided between this track and 'Still Raining, Still Dreaming'. Initially, it introduced the brilliant suite of music which segued into...

1983... (A MERMAN I SHOULD TURN TO BE)

Delicate guitar passages established a mood

that mixed psychedelic rock and jazz, before Hendrix began to paint in words the portrait of a world torn by war and despair, from which the only escape is the sea. Playing all the instruments apart from flute (supplied by Chris Wood of Traffic, the third band member to guest on this album), Jimi created an orchestral tapestry of sound, which flowed elegantly into a gentle chaos of tape effects, backwards guitar, and chiming percussion, and then to...

MOON, TURN THE TIDES... GENTLY, GENTLY AWAY

Multi-dubbed guitar motifs restored the psychedelic jazz feel, vamping melodically for several minutes until the mood became almost frenzied, and shifted into an electronically treated drum solo. At last, the familiar themes of '1983' re-emerged, to guide the suite to its conclusion, and complete 20 minutes of stunningly complex and beautiful instrumental tonalities. These two tracks were taped in a single remarkable session, on April 23, 1968.

STILL RAINING, STILL DREAMING

Still jamming, too, first through another verse of 'Rainy Day, Dream Away', and then into a coda which gradually wound down the mellow jazz groove of the original track.

HOUSE BURNING DOWN

Another collaboration between Jimi and Mitch (Noel Redding played on just five 'Electric Ladyland' songs), 'House Burning Down' twisted through several key changes in its tight, swirling intro, and then shifted again as the strident chorus moved into the reportorial verses. Like so many of Jimi's songs from this period, there was an atmosphere of impending doom in the air, inspired by the outburst of black-on-black violence that had shaken some of America's ghettos earlier in 1968. "Try to learn instead of burn", Jimi advised hopefully, before (as ever) finding salvation somewhere other than the land – this time via a friendly visitor from another galaxy.

ALL ALONG THE WATCHTOWER

'I Dreamed I Saw St. Augustine' was Hendrix's first choice of material when he listened to Bob Dylan's 'John Wesley Harding' for the first time. In 1970, he recorded another song from the set, 'Drifter's Escape'; but his arrangement of 'All Along The Watchtower' was so convincing that Dylan himself has been using it ever since.

In its original acoustic form, Dylan threw the emphasis of the song on its apocalyptic imagery. Hendrix used the sound of the studio to evoke the storms and the sense of dread, creating an echoed aural landscape that remains the most successful Dylan cover ever recorded. Dave Mason of Traffic contributed bass and acoustic guitar to the basic session on January 21, 1968; Jimi completed his overdubs four months later, and the song subsequently became a worldwide hit single.

VOODOO CHILE (SLIGHT RETURN)

Two days after recording the epic 'Voodoo Chile', Jimi was back at the Record Plant, with Mitch and Noel, ready for this 'Slight Return'. What evolved, over eight takes, was the single most impressive piece of guitar-playing I've ever heard, on a track that compresses every ounce of Hendrix's ambition, musical technique, production skill and uncanny sense of impending disaster within five minutes. From its opening wah-wah chatter to the wails of feedback that bring the song to its close, it's an extravaganza of noise and naked emotion. Its verbal imagery is ablaze with destruction and imminent death; and the music is equal to every last nuance. By its very nature, feedback evokes loss of control: during this performance, Hendrix handles it like a wizard controlling a hurricane.

HENDRIX

BAND OF GYPSYS

BAND OF GYPSYS

When Chas Chandler first began to manage Jimi Hendrix, he quickly discovered that Jimi had left his signature on a bewildering array of record, publishing and management contracts over the previous three years. Chas scampered around New York buying up the contracts, but Jimi neglected to mention the small matter of an exclusive recording deal that he'd signed his name to on October 15, 1965. The contract required that Jimi would, for the next three years, "produce and play and/or sing exclusively for PPX Enterprises", a New York production company headed by one Ed Chalpin (see the Unofficial CDs section for more on PPX, and Jimi's links with the company via singer Curtis Knight).

The PPX deal was hardly lucrative: it entitled Jimi to a 1% royalty after all the company's costs had been paid. But it was legally binding, and by signing to Polydor and Warner/Reprise, Jimi had broken it. Writs cascaded in all directions, until in the summer of 1968 Ed Chalpin (now sheltering under Capitol Records' wings) was offered a settlement by Warner/Reprise, which entitled him to the rights to issue Jimi's next album of new material, plus royalties on the first three Experience LPs.

Meanwhile, Warner/Reprise were berating Hendrix for the late delivery of their next album. To ease the pressure, Jimi's manager, Mike Jeffery, suggested that Jimi present Chalpin and Capitol with a live record. To that end, and that end only, Jeffery encouraged Hendrix to assemble a new band as swiftly as possible. And so was born The Band Of Gypsys.

Like The Experience, the new line-up was a trio, teaming Hendrix with his longtime friend, bassist Billy Cox, and the extrovert ex-Electric Flag drummer Buddy Miles. "We got together to help Jimi out, because he couldn't find anybody else to do it," explained Billy Cox. "With a lot of the music we did, I think Jimi was frustrated because he had a lot of pressure on him. He was being pushed all the time." That frustration began in the studio, where the trio (often augmented by other musicians) made faltering progress towards the Warner/Reprise album. And it carried over to the stage on New Year's Eve 1969 and New Year's Day 1970, when The Band Of Gypsys played their first live shows at the Fillmore East in New York.

Six songs – four written by Hendrix, two by the over-enthusiastic Miles – were presented to Capitol early in 1970 as the 'Band Of Gypsys' album. Ed Chalpin hated it, and so indeed did Hendrix: "I wasn't too satisfied with the album," he admitted shortly after its release. "If it had been up to me, I would have never put it out. Not enough preparation went into it." But Jimi's artistic judgement counted for little against the legal obligation to Capitol, which 'Band Of Gypsys' satisfied. The album went Top 10 in Britain and America, regardless of its merits.

Tentative and uncomfortable, the original 'Band Of Gypsys' was scarcely a competent record of the Fillmore East gigs, let alone a decent Hendrix album. But its leanings towards a rock/funk crossover indicated at least one of the musical directions he'd been exploring in recent months, and the recruitment of his first all-black band since he'd met Chas Chandler did improve his standing among radical black activists.

BAND OF GYPSYS
(VERSION 1)
LP RELEASE: POLYDOR/TRACK 2406 002 (USA), JUNE 1970

CD RELEASE: POLYDOR 821 933-2 (GERMANY), MAY 1988
Tracks: Who Knows/Machine Gun/Changes/ Power To Love/Message Of Love/We Gotta Live Together

The original Polydor CD release was typical of their lack of attention to detail: the sound quality was murky, and the credits suggested that all six songs had been recorded on December 31, 1969, whereas they actually came from the following day's shows.

Students of the macabre might consider tracking down the Japanese CD edition of 'Band Of Gypsys' (Polydor P20P-22006), as this uses the original 'puppet' cover prepared for the first pressing of the UK LP in 1970. Pressure from Mike Jeffery forced Track Records to alter the artwork later that year, but nobody told the Japanese.

BAND OF GYPSYS
(VERSION 2)

CD RELEASE: POLYDOR 847 237-2 (GERMANY), 1993

Tracks: Who Knows/Machine Gun/Changes/ Power Of Love/Message To Love/We Gotta Live Together/Hear My Train/Foxy Lady/Stop

In 1986, Alan Douglas issued 'Band Of Gypsys 2', a misbegotten vinyl-only release that never appeared outside America. In fact, two versions of this LP were released, albeit with one set of cover artwork, making it impossible to distinguish the two at first glance.

The major problem with Douglas's creation was that only three of the tracks from the album actually featured The Band Of Gypsys: the rest came from Berkeley and Atlanta shows in 1970, featuring the revamped Experience.

In 1991, the three authentic BOG songs were added to the original six when the CD was included in the 'Footlights' boxed set. Meanwhile, the six-song edition remained in the shops. In 1992, Douglas explained that the revamped 'Band Of Gypsys' wasn't available separately because he wanted to change it again: "I found four more new tracks. We have three that have never been released, including

a very good 'Stepping Stone', and we have all four 'Machine Guns'. I'm trying to get Capitol to sit down and forget everything that's happened and we'll pick the best tracks and make the best of it."

What happened next? In 1993, the 1991 edition of 'Band Of Gypsys' appeared on CD in its own right, with the ridiculous claim that it "contains 3 previously unreleased tracks". No 'Stepping Stone', no new 'Machine Gun'; just more egg on the Estate's collective face. To compound the mistakes, the titles of two of the songs were mistakenly altered; and a third was listed with the wrong composer. The bad karma surrounding 'Band Of Gypsys' continues to this day.

TRACK-BY-TRACK:

WHO KNOWS

With The Band Of Gypsys, Jimi had to balance the energetic enthusiasm of Buddy Miles' playing against his tendency to turn every song into a vocal call-and-response routine with the audience. The mid-tempo solidity of 'Who Knows' typified the fluency of Hendrix's playing at these shows, and the low level of inspiration involved in the songwriting. But most of all it demonstrated the chasm between Jimi's soul and Buddy's showbiz – one self-effacing, the other almost exhibitionistic.

MACHINE GUN

Whether you regarded it as a comment on the Vietnam conflict, or a wider outburst of grief and anger at the racial divide, 'Machine Gun' inspired some of Hendrix's most majestic and anguished guitar work. Note after sustained note was mutated into a deathly, screaming howl, while Miles brought a martial air to his drum patterns, and Billy Cox toyed with a bass riff similar to Cream's 'Sunshine Of Your Love'. This performance alone legitimised the existence of The Band Of Gypsys.

CHANGES

Sometimes known as 'Them Changes', this was the first of Miles' songs on the album – little more than a lightweight Stax soul riff, to be honest, topped with a melody line that stretched Buddy's voice to the limit. Jimi's involvement was restricted to layering wah-wah guitar across the chorus.

POWER OF SOUL

It was listed as 'Power To Love' on the first CD, 'Power Of Love' on the second, 'With The Power' on a later compilation, and often introduced in concert by Jimi as either 'Crash Landing' or 'Paper Airplanes'. But the 'correct' title comes from the chorus line, which sums up the song's message: "with the power of soul/anything is possible". Deliberately understated, the song downplayed Hendrix's guitar theatrics to leave the lyrical thrust in the foreground.

MESSAGE TO LOVE

This song also went through a change of title: it's listed on the first CD release as 'Message Of Love'. Its theme was the same as its predecessor, but it lacked the subtle touch of 'Power Of Soul', and never really broke out of its vague funk origins to become a fully-fledged song.

WE GOTTA LIVE TOGETHER

Hendrix gifted this second Buddy Miles tune with some astonishing guitar playing, as free-flowing and ambitious as anything on the album. But like too much of 'Band Of

Gypsys', the song was a genre exercise in funk-soul, rather than a composition that boasted any unique reason for its existence. It brought the original album to a downbeat close.

HEAR MY TRAIN A-COMIN'

The first of the bonus cuts on the second CD release of 'Band Of Gypsys' is introduced by Jimi as "a slow blues... 'Lonesome Train', we can call it that". It's better known as 'Hear My Train A-Comin' ' or 'Getting My Heart Back Together Again', under which titles it became a key piece in Hendrix's repertoire from 1967 until his death. Like 'Red House' before it, the song's standard blues imagery allowed him to use it as an all-purpose barometer of his emotional involvement, some nights throwing it away with a sly flourish, others treating it as the vehicle for confessional soul singing and devastating guitar work.

The Band Of Gypsys' version, the only song on this CD from the New Year's Eve shows, belongs firmly in the latter category: it's a prime example of guitar fireworks, that quickly moves beyond theatrics into a compelling intensity.

FOXY LADY

The final numbers on the revised CD were both taken from video-tapes of the shows, with all the inferior sound quality that implies. No song demonstrates more clearly than 'Foxy Lady' the technical gulf between Mitch Mitchell's experimental, jazz-tinged drumming, and the leaden time-keeping of Buddy Miles. At his worst, Buddy often undercut the natural rhythm of the song: where Mitch would have fired Hendrix into some hot guitar playing, Miles forced him to concentrate on merely keeping the band from collapsing.

STOP

The CD credits Miles as the author of this New York soul song, but it was actually written by Jerry Ragavoy and Mort Shuman, and had already been adopted by Mike Bloomfield and Al Kooper for their 'Supersession' album. Hendrix played valiantly again on this cut, but the band let him down: maybe it's a blessing that this leaden, sonically-challenged performance fades out before its conclusion.

SECTION 2

THE POSTHUMOUS ALBUMS

Jimi Hendrix's final day in New York climaxed with the official opening of his Electric Lady Studio. He left the party early; he never entered a recording studio again.

Two days later, on August 28, 1970, Jimi Hendrix gave an interview to *Melody Maker* journalist Roy Hollingworth. "I've given this era of music everything," he said. "I still sound the same, my music's the same, and I can't think of anything new to add to it in its present state. This era of music, sparked off by The Beatles, has come to an end. Something new has got to come and Jimi Hendrix will be there.

"I want a big band. I don't mean three harps and fourteen violins. I mean a big band full of competent musicians that I can conduct and write for. And with the music we will paint pictures of earth and space, so that the listener can be taken somewhere."

Three weeks later, Hendrix was dead. He left behind him scores of tape reels, stuffed full of jams, half-finished masters, demos,,jokes, sketches for compositions in progress, layers of interlocked guitar overdubs. On paper and on tape, he'd laid out the skeleton of an autobiographical song cycle called 'Black Gold'. More openly, he had spoken to many of his friends and associates about his plans for his next album, a double-LP to be called 'The First Rays Of The New Rising Sun'.

It was never released; neither was 'Black Gold'. But Hendrix's career as a posthumous recording star was just beginning. His death was the signal for everyone who owned a piece of studio tape bearing his music to cash in their chips. For the next five years, the market was flooded with unauthorised albums, carrying similar material to the 'Unofficial CDs' covered in Section 3 of this book.

Those worthless exercises in exploitation queered the pitch for the 'official' Hendrix release schedule, which began just a few weeks after Jimi's demise, paused briefly in the late Seventies, and then gradually picked up steam after 1980.

In the immediate aftermath of his death, there was an insistent demand for 'new' Hendrix product. His first posthumous album came close to topping the British and American charts, while the uncompromisingly brilliant guitar extravaganza that was 'Voodoo Child (Slight Return)' actually reached No. 1 on the UK singles chart in the final weeks of 1970.

But very quickly the law of diminishing returns assumed command, both commercially and artistically. By the mid-Seventies, the audience for the increasingly unsatisfactory albums being issued under Hendrix's name was rapidly disintegrating into a vocal core of fans, who began to swap concert tapes and dream that one day 'Black Gold' would magically be transformed from myth into reality.

The final straw for many Hendrix followers was the overdubbing of his original tapes for two mid-Seventies albums – not simply because his tracks were being tampered with, but because project supremo Alan Douglas had chosen not to use Jimi's original sidemen to carry out the repairs.

Douglas, who had worked with Jimi on several musical concepts in 1969 and 1970, gradually assumed command over Jimi's entire catalogue, however. After one more dip into the treasure-house of unissued tapes in 1980, he spent the next few years preparing a series of compilations, which were decorated with the minimum of unheard live material. The late Eighties release of albums like 'Live At Winterland' and 'Radio One' denoted a new openness in his philosophy, but it's true to say that even the most spectacular of Douglas's releases since then have still fallen short of finding universal acceptance. Fans still demand the impossible; Douglas presents them with naked commercial regard, sometimes presented as altruism. Two steps forward, three steps back, as Vladimir Ilyich put it.

THE CRY OF LOVE

LP RELEASE: TRACK 2408 101 (UK), MARCH 1971
CD RELEASE: POLYDOR 829 926-2 (UK), MARCH 1989
CD REISSUED ON POLYDOR 847 242-2 (UK), C. 1992

Tracks: Freedom/Drifting/Ezy Ryder/Night Bird Flying/My Friend/Straight Ahead/Astro Man/Angel/In From The Storm/Belly Button Window

THE ALBUM: It was presented as Jimi's final album, as though there had never been any debate about its contents. But drummer Mitch Mitchell (who added some subtle overdubs to various tracks) and engineer Eddie Kramer, the co-compilers of 'The Cry Of Love', were working to a game plan of their own design. They chose to ignore both the title and the planned format (a double-LP set, remember) of 'The First Rays Of The New Rising Sun'. They also omitted the virtual title track of Jimi's grandiose project, 'Hey Baby (The Land Of The New Rising Sun)', plus songs like 'Dolly Dagger' (introduced by Hendrix at the Isle of Wight as "a song we're trying to get together for our next album"), 'Midnight Lightning' and 'Room Full Of Mirrors', all of which Mitch had been playing on stage with Jimi in the months leading up to his death.

In many ways, the second posthumous album, the pretend soundtrack LP 'Rainbow Bridge', actually came closer to realising Hendrix's dream of 'New Rising Sun' than did 'The Cry Of Love'. But it's likely that Mitch and Eddie's sole aim was to produce a commercial album as quickly as possible, to satisfy the demands of both Jimi's audience and his record company – who were no doubt relieved that the double-LP had been chopped down to a single record.

For all that, 'The Cry Of Love' (the name Jimi gave his band on his spring 1970 US tour) was a disappointingly subdued affair – more inspired than 'Band Of Gypsys', it's true, but scarcely on a level with the sonic and artistic invention of 'Electric Ladyland'. In its current form, it adds weight to those who suggest that Hendrix had run into some kind of musical block in the months up to his death.

The earliest song on the album was also the least comfortable – the stoned blues 'My Friend', which dated back to the sessions for 'Electric Ladyland' in June 1968, and apparently featured Stephen Stills on piano. Another song, 'Ezy Ryder', came from the ill-fated attempt to cut a Band of Gypsys studio

LP in December 1969. Chris Wood and Steve Winwood of Traffic guested on this riff-led rocker, with which Hendrix had been toying since early in 1969.

The remaining songs all emanated from the 'New Rising Sun' sessions of June to August 1970, with Mitch Mitchell on drums and Billy Cox on bass. 'Freedom' was the 'blackest' song on the album, an anthem for the times powered by Sly Stone-style backing vocals. 'Straight Ahead' walked a similar tightrope between rock and soul. But the most effective songs on the record were the ballads – the moving 'Angel', which Jimi had written early in 1968, inspired by a dream about his late mother; and 'Drifting', which developed through a flurry of backwards guitar and a fragile vocal that teetered on the brink of collapse.

Two other numbers were apparently taken from the mysterious (and still, in the mid-90s, unreleased) 'Black Gold' suite – 'Astro Man', with its unfortunate references to "that old faggot Superman", and the solo performance of 'Belly Button Window'. Cut during Jimi's final studio session, it returned him to his mother's womb, fruitlessly searching for a reason to enter the world. Suicide theorists seized on the song as ammunition for their case. The defence could enter 'In From The Storm' as evidence: here, as at the Isle Of Wight, it stood as a gesture of defiance against the forces that had stymied his progress in recent months.

THE CD: As it's not regarded as an 'official' Hendrix album, 'The Cry Of Love' hasn't undergone the full remastering process allotted to Jimi's earlier records. There are two UK versions of the disc, both with a minimalist booklet that credits 'Jimmi Hendrix' as co-producer, and has him writing "helly my friend" in the liner-note poem.

The earlier CD transfer succeeded in clipping off the first chord of 'Freedom'; the second edition isn't perfect, but has clearer, louder and more exciting sound quality.

ISLE OF WIGHT

LP RELEASE: POLYDOR 2302 016 (UK), NOVEMBER 1971

CD RELEASE: POLYDOR 831 313-2 (UK), MARCH 1989

Tracks: Midnight Lightnin'/Foxy Lady/Lover Man/Freedom/All Along The Watchtower/In From The Storm

The 'Woodstock' movie was released a couple of months before Jimi Hendrix appeared as the star attraction at the third Isle of Wight festival – his last scheduled concert in Britain. 'Woodstock', with its carefully edited clip of Jimi's finest minutes at the 1969 festival, aroused impossible expectations of his UK visit, and the live set offered by Hendrix, Billy Cox and Mitch Mitchell never came close to meeting them.

Jimi's death less than three weeks later altered public perceptions of the show, and excited a demand for a live album from this 'farewell' performance. 'Isle Of Wight' was hastily assembled to satisfy this enthusiasm, but it was never issued in America – proof that Jimi's estate regarded it as a souvenir of a British event, not a full-scale Hendrix album.

In fact, engineer Eddie Kramer, asked by Jimi's manager Mike Jeffery to concoct an album from the festival tapes, took one listen and flatly refused. Instead, the task was handed to a British engineer, Carlos Ohlms. "I thought the album was awful," Kramer explained. "While I couldn't stop its release, I told Jeffery that under no circumstances was my name to be credited or associated with it in any way."

It was a sensible request on Kramer's part, as the Polydor LP granted Jimi's memory few favours. It ran to just 34 minutes, offering two classics from his back catalogue, two songs from 'The Cry Of Love', and two previously unreleased. One of those was 'Midnight Lightning', a stodgy blues-rocker which never caught fire, and also suffered from walkie-talkie announcements being picked up by Jimi's amps. It segued naturally into an equally uninspired 'Foxy Lady', and then a chaotic, if frenetic, 'Lover Man'.

A brilliant arrangement of 'Freedom', with Hendrix reworking the tired studio version into an almost orchestrated set of riffs and runs, lifted the gloom, before a scrappy 'All Along The Watchtower' reversed the balance. The album, and the gig, ended heroically, as Mitch Mitchell's drum solo led into a passionate 'In From The Storm', Hendrix redeeming some dignity and power from a concert in which he knew he had failed. The extent of his failure only became apparent in 1991, when a home-video and then a second CD, 'Live Isle Of Wight '70', were pulled from the wreckage.

THE CD: Like its vinyl counterpart, the 'Isle Of Wight' CD wasn't issued in America, leaving European and Japanese editions as the only ones on the market. The common German pressing is as painful as the original album, presented with a one-sided sheet of paper instead of a booklet. There's no mention of Mitch Mitchell or Billy Cox anywhere in the package.

RAINBOW BRIDGE

LP RELEASE: REPRISE K 41459 (UK), NOVEMBER 1971

CD RELEASE: REPRISE K 2231459 (JAPAN), MARCH 1987

Tracks: Dolly Dagger/Earth Blues/Pali Gap/Room Full Of Mirrors/Star Spangled Banner/Look Over Yonder/Hear My Train A-Comin'/Hey Baby (New Rising Sun)

THE ALBUM: Why? Why was 'Rainbow Bridge' so much more impressive than 'The Cry Of Love'? Why did it purport to be a film soundtrack album, when it had only a few minutes of music from the film? And why has it never been released on CD in Britain or America?

The release of the uninspired 'Experience' film soundtrack earlier in 1971 (see the Unofficial CDs section) wasn't exactly an ideal precedent for this album. Even less convincing was the movie itself, which tacked around 20 minutes of Hendrix live performance from on top of a Hawaiian volcano (known as Rainbow Ridge, not Bridge) with more than an hour of tortuous, inane hippie psycho-babble. No-one who'd watched the movie on anything less mind-altering than acid would have considered buying the album for a second.

The entire deal was Mike Jeffery's way of establishing his counter-culture credentials, by letting film-maker Chuck Wein inveigle Jimi and band into his ridiculous movie. Jeffery agreed to furnish Warner Brothers films with a soundtrack album, only to discover after Jimi's death that the Hawaii performance hadn't been adequately recorded. (As an example, Mitch Mitchell had to re-dub all his drum parts for the movie, the original track being unusable.)

With the assistance of Eddie Kramer, Mike Jeffery finally assembled an album that dragged every possible contender from a variety of tape sources – several of the songs having been pulled from the pool of material Jimi had been stockpiling for 'The First Rays Of The New Rising Sun'. But although this haphazard approach was far from foolproof, it did unearth some recordings that evoked Jimi's dream of a rock/soul crossover far more successfully than the rather laboured 'The Cry Of Love'.

The oldest song on the album was 'Look Over Yonder' (alias 'Mr Bad Luck', under which title Jimi had been performing it since the pre-Experience days of 1966). He'd cut a studio version with Noel Redding and Mitch Mitchell in May 1967, but the R&B-flavoured 'Rainbow Bridge' take hailed from the post-Electric Ladyland sessions of October 1968.

'Star-Spangled Banner' aroused great expectations from those who'd seen the 'Woodstock' movie, but the March 1969 studio take was an abomination alongside that epochal rendition. Cloaked in double-speed guitar overdubs, it was passionless, synthesised and almost unlistenable.

Everything else on the album came from the last year of Hendrix's life. 'Earth Blues' (with The Ronettes, no less, on backing vocals) and 'Room Full Of Mirrors' were cut during the abortive Band Of Gypsys studio sessions around Christmas 1969, and perfectly illustrated the modest ambitions of the Hendrix/Miles/Cox line-up. Three further songs were pulled from July 1970 sessions featuring Cox and Mitchell, including the virtual title song of the album Jimi was trying to complete when he died, 'Hey Baby (New Rising Sun)', the sparkling 'Dolly Dagger', a riff-rocker dedicated to girlfriend Devon Wilson, and the instrumental 'Pali Gap' – named by Mike Jeffery in a vain attempt to give the LP some Hawaiian ambience.

Ironically, the finest performance on 'Rainbow Bridge' wasn't a studio cut at all, but a song from the Berkeley shows in May 1970 that would also supply some stellar moments to the next album, 'Hendrix In The West'. 'Hear My Train A-Comin' ' supplanted 'Red House' as Jimi's ultimate expression of the blues in his final year, and this is undoubtedly the definitive rendition – a ten-minute exercise in "less is more", in direct contrast to the over-egged trickery of 'Star-Spangled Banner'. For this track alone, Rainbow Bridge has to be heard.

THE CD: Unlike the rest of the original 1970s posthumous albums, 'Rainbow Bridge' has only been issued on CD in Japan – and even then it was available for a mere matter of months.

There is, however, a bootleg CD of the album, also hailing from Japan, which includes the original LP, plus five bonus cuts, taken from official Band Of Gypsys' singles.

HENDRIX IN THE WEST

LP RELEASE: POLYDOR 2301 018 (UK), JANUARY 1972
CD RELEASE: POLYDOR 831 312-2 (UK), FEBRUARY 1989
Tracks: Johnny B. Goode/Lover Man/Blue Suede Shoes/Voodoo Child (Slight Return)/God Save The Queen/Sgt. Pepper's Lonely Hearts Club Band/Little Wing/Red House

THE ALBUM: Alongside the archive excavations which produced the studio albums, 'The Cry Of Love' and 'Rainbow Bridge', Mike Jeffery and Eddie Kramer had been considering the possibility of issuing a live album taken from Jimi's two shows at the Community

Theater in Berkeley, California, on May 30, 1970. Kramer actually mastered the full tapes of both shows, while the visual record of the concert was duly issued as a movie entitled 'Jimi Plays Berkeley' in late 1971. But Kramer decided that the concerts didn't justify LP release in their own right, and the decision to include the Berkeley performance of 'Hear My Train A-Comin' ' on the 'Rainbow Bridge' LP finally scuppered plans for the live set.

In its place, Kramer picked the best remaining tracks from Berkeley, and combined them with performances from other 1969 and 1970 live shows. The three gigs immediately available to them were the Royal Albert Hall, London, from February 24, 1969; the San Diego Sports Arena, from May 24, 1969; and the Isle of Wight festival, on August 30, 1970.

So far so good; but there were legal problems regarding the ownership of the Albert Hall tapes, which had already been raided by Ember Records for the release of the 'Experience' LP (see the introduction to the Unofficial CDs section of this book for more details). Mike Jeffery hit upon a strange solution: using the Albert Hall tracks, but pretending that they came from San Diego. 'Voodoo

Child (Slight Return)' and 'Little Wing' were deliberately miscredited, an idea that worked brilliantly until the rival claimants to the Albert Hall material actually listened to 'Hendrix In The West', whereupon they slapped a lawsuit on Jeffery and his cohorts.

Those antics aside, most of 'Hendrix In The West' was a worthy tribute, and some of it was brilliant. For guitar theatrics, Jimi never topped the apparently impromptu Berkeley rendition of Chuck Berry's 'Johnny B. Goode'. When I first heard it as a kid, I assumed that there were three guitarists on the record, and I was still impressed. It has to be heard – or seen, via 'Jimi Plays Berkeley' – to be believed.

The album leaps straight into a best-ever rendition of 'Lover Man', Jimi's revamp of the blues standard 'Rock Me Baby'. It's another Berkeley cut – but then so is the appallingly lame 'Blue Suede Shoes', from the pre-show rehearsals, which is to 'Johnny B. Goode' what a snail is to a cheetah. The snail's probably prettier, too.

The first disguised Albert Hall cut, 'Voodoo Child (Slight Return)', is in a different league, as Hendrix comes close to matching the multi-dubbed soundscapes of the studio take with a single six-stringed instrument. Another descent into bathos follows, with the Isle Of Wight intro of 'God Save The Queen'/'Sgt. Pepper' – no 'Star-Spangled Banner' this. Then back to the Albert Hall for a poignantly beautiful 'Little Wing', which for sensitivity and technique cuts the 'Axis' studio cut dead; and finally a genuine relic from San Diego, in the shape of a long, complex 'Red House', as close to definitive as any live reading of the song.

THE CD: Like the album, the CD continued to insist that no Albert Hall tapes were included. Of all the Polydor CDs issued in Britain, this proves the most difficult to track down; one of these days, Alan Douglas will reissue 'The Cry Of Love', 'Rainbow Bridge' and the best of this record on one set, and we'll all die happy.

Or not.

WAR HEROES

LP RELEASE: POLYDOR 2302 020 (UK), OCTOBER 1972
CD RELEASE: POLYDOR 813 573-2 (UK), MARCH 1989

Tracks: Bleeding Heart/Highway Chile/Tax Free/Peter Gunn Catastrophe/Stepping Stone/Midnight/3 Little Bears/Beginning/Izabella

THE ALBUM: 'War Heroes'? The title of this ragbag of Hendrix leftovers owed more to the date of its release, at the height of anti-Vietnam feeling in America, than any relevance to its contents.

With the aid of engineer Eddie Kramer, Mike Jeffery assembled what was promoted as the first album of Jimi's out-takes, rather than the supposedly complete tracks that were included on 'The Cry Of Love' and 'Rainbow Bridge'. Three tracks, at least, had been approved by Hendrix: 'Highway Chile' was the flipside of 'The Wind Cries Mary', while 'Stepping Stone'/'Izabella' was a Band Of Gypsys single, admittedly pulled from the shops within days of its release. Both those rather tentative rock/funk crossovers were remixed for 'War Heroes', while Mitch Mitchell replaced Buddy Miles' original drum part on 'Stepping Stone'.

For the rest of the album, the compilers had to wade through a variety of session tapes, covering more than two years. There were two out-takes from 'Electric Ladyland': the instrumental 'Tax Free' (written by the Swedish duo Hansson & Karlsson, who taught it to Jimi during an after-hours Stockholm jam in

September 1967); and the cod reggae tune '3 Little Bears', on which Jimi delivered his own verdict early in the proceedings: "I don't know if I can go through with this, it's really silly."

Noel Redding's 'Midnight', an instrumental riff in 'Foxy Lady' vein, came from The Experience's last batch of sessions in April 1969, while Elmore James' 'Bleeding Heart' was another Band Of Gypsys outing. Hendrix had been performing the song since at least 1965, and an earlier studio cut was included on the ':Blues' CD in 1994.

The remaining tracks dated from the summer of 1970: 'Beginning', better known from its Woodstock appearance as 'Jam Back At The House', was a Mitch Mitchell composition, though Hendrix virtually claimed it as his own with an intense solo; while the aptly named 'Peter Gunn Catastrophe' saw Hendrix, Mitchell and Billy Cox cruising through Henry Mancini's Peter Gunn TV theme, before collapsing into a parody of the Frankie Laine hit 'Jealousy'. With this track and '3 Little Bears' on board, the good ship 'War Heroes' was sailing through treacherous waters – and the worldwide sales of the album were disappointing.

THE CD: Packaged with the bare minimum of (often erroneous) information, 'War Heroes' needs a revamp. 'Bleeding Heart' and 'Midnight' are wrongly credited as Hendrix songs; and there are no musician credits or recording dates. The disc lists different titles for two songs to those on the back cover. Worst of all, the spine of the CD credits someone called 'Jimmi Hendrix'.

LOOSE ENDS

LP RELEASE: POLYDOR 2310 301 (UK), FEBRUARY 1974
CD RELEASE: POLYDOR 837 574-2 (UK), MARCH 1989

Tracks: Coming Down Hard On Me Baby/Blue Suede Shoes/Jam 292/The Stars That Play With Laughing Sam's Dice/Drifter's Escape/Burning Desire/I'm Your Hoochie Coochie Man/Electric Ladyland

THE ALBUM: At least the title was honest. Eddie Kramer didn't want any more part in the discrediting of Hendrix's reputation: his assistant engineer, John Jansen, told author John McDermott: "Mike Jeffery kept pressing for 'just one more'. Anything that remotely sounded like music was worth going to Polydor, and getting money for an album."

In his book, *Setting The Record Straight*, McDermott describes 'Loose Ends' as "a callous and shameful exercise". He's not wrong. It's undoubtedly the worst album officially approved by the curators of the Hendrix legacy, and it's impossible to imagine that Jimi would have wanted the public to hear a single second of it.

The one exception to that rule is the one track that Jimi himself released, the 1967 B-side 'The Stars That Play With Laughing Sam's Dice'. As a twist of fate, this mix of the song is infinitely preferable to the abomination issued on the 'Smash Hits' CD: it's in stereo, for a start, and the mix is clearer, louder, sharper and more listenable. It's a wonderful performance, too – a mind-altering journey in concept and sound.

Only one other song on 'Loose Ends' deserves that acclaim – virtually a solo rendition (Buddy Miles' drums were wiped) of 'Electric Ladyland', recorded after the version on the album of that title, and emphasising Jimi's debt to Curtis Mayfield's guitar playing. Its 92 seconds of beauty follow more than 15 minutes of turgid Band Of Gypsys jamming, as Hendrix, Miles and Cox plod through the lacklustre 'Burning Desire' and make equally heavy weight of 'Hoochie Coochie Man'.

Equally appalling is 'Blue Suede Shoes', a four-minute Band Of Gypsys track which comprises less than two minutes of song and far too much studio badinage. If you want to hear Jimi joking around with 'Heartbreak Hotel', here's where you come. Just be grateful that Mike Jeffery didn't insist on the inclusion of the full 11-minute jam from which this sorry track was pulled.

Hendrix's arrangements of Bob Dylan's 'Like A Rolling Stone' (at Monterey) and 'All Along The Watchtower' (on 'Electric Ladyland') might whet the appetite for another Dylan cover, 'Drifter's Escape'. But this May 1970 recording, one of the first at Jimi's own Electric Lady studio, smothers the song in musical clutter, subduing its original acoustic rhythms beneath the chatter of funk guitars. Two months later, the same musicians rambled through the blues-soul of 'Come Down Hard On Me', an undeveloped and certainly not complete song in the making.

By far the least enticing title on 'Loose Ends' was 'Jam 292', named by Jeffery after its studio tape number. Ironically, though, this impromptu mix of blues structure and wah-wah guitar, with Hendrix accompanied by Stephen Stills and drummer Dallas Taylor, was one of the album's most impressive tracks. It was still little more than inconsequential, however, which is an apt summary of the entire record.

THE CD: Given only the most cursory of remastering jobs, 'Loose Ends' also suffers from appalling cover design, erroneous credits (no mention of Stills and Taylor, for instance, and 'Hoochie Coochie Man' given the wrong composer and title) and a complete lack of annotation.

SOUNDTRACK RECORDINGS FROM THE FILM 'JIMI HENDRIX'

LP RELEASE: REPRISE K 64017 (UK), JUNE 1973
UNISSUED ON CD

Tracks: Rock Me Baby/Wild Thing/Machine Gun/Johnny B. Goode/Hey Joe/Purple Haze/Like A Rolling Stone/Star Spangled Banner/Machine Gun/Hear My Train A-Comin'/Red House/In From The Storm plus interviews

THE ALBUM: Essentially a live 'greatest hits' set, taken from the tapes in professional circulation at the time the album was released, this double-LP accompanied *A Film About Jimi Hendrix* – the excellent (for the period) documentary movie assembled by Joe Boyd. Alongside many of the interview clips used in the film, the album contained 'Rock Me Baby', 'Wild Thing', 'Hey Joe' and 'Like A Rolling Stone' from Monterey in June 1967 (all available on the 'Jimi Plays Monterey' CD); the beautiful acoustic 'Hear My Train A-Comin' ' from December 1967 (now available on the ':Blues' CD); 'Star Spangled Banner' from Woodstock in 1969; 'Machine Gun' from the 'Band Of Gypsys' album; 'Johnny B. Goode' from Berkeley in May 1970 (as heard on 'Hendrix In The West'); 'Purple Haze' from the same show; and 'In From The Storm', 'Red House' and 'Machine Gun' from the Isle Of Wight in August 1970 (all available on the CDs of that concert).

Aside from the interviews, only 'Purple Haze' isn't currently available on an official CD release – which is presumably why this set hasn't been issued as a compact disc.

CRASH LANDING

LP RELEASE: POLYDOR 2310 398 (UK), AUGUST 1975

CD RELEASE: POLYDOR 827 932-2 (UK), MARCH 1989

Tracks: Message To Love/Somewhere Over The Rainbow/Crash Landing/Coming Down Hard On Me Baby/Peace In Mississippi/With The Power/Stone Free/MLK

THE ALBUM: Jimi Hendrix first approached Alan Douglas, entrepreneur and jazz label boss, in September 1969. Douglas attended one of Jimi's most chaotic studio sessions, after which the guitarist told him that he needed help to supervise his projects, and prevent his recording attempts from being overrun by well-wishers, hangers-on and more nefarious characters.

Douglas and Hendrix remained in some kind of contact for the remaining year of Jimi's life, but Alan was sidelined by Mike Jeffery's dominance over the first three years of posthumous releases. Jeffery's death in a March 1973 plane crash, in circumstances that many regarded as sinister, opened the gates for new curators to take control of Jimi's artistic legacy. Douglas had financed the recording of several Hendrix jams, and as the owner of unissued material he was approached by Warner Brothers after Jeffery's demise in the hope that he could provide the label with something that could be salvaged for commercial release. Given this window of opportunity, Douglas began to investigate other possible tape sources. He unearthed a quantity of unfinished recordings made at the Record Plant in New York, which he reckoned were possible contenders for release.

According to John McDermott, he laid out the running order for an album he titled 'Crash Landing', which would feature: 'Crash Landing', 'Somewhere', 'With The Power', 'New Rising Sun', 'Message To Love', an untitled jam, 'Stone Free', 'Peace In Mississippi' and 'Here Comes Your Lover Man'. Listening back to the tapes, though, Douglas realised that the ensemble playing of The Band Of Gypsys, The Experience and the Cry Of Love band was too shambolic for release in its current state.

So he took the tapes, and the problem, to top studio engineer Tony Bongiovi. The two men agreed on a solution, albeit an endlessly controversial one: the original tapes should not only be remixed but also overdubbed by session musicians, to approximate the musical vision inherent but dormant within the existing tracks.

In many cases, Bongiovi and Douglas were working on material already rejected by Eddie Kramer and John Jansen. But the latter pair had started from the idea that they would simply be transferring the best of Hendrix's work from master-tape to record. The new régime had more ambitious and creative work in mind.

Their involvement was certainly painstaking. This was no haphazard overdubbing of impromptu bass and drum parts. Instead, Bongiovi assembled every possible take of each song, and reviewed their potential for cannibalising. Guitar solos were extracted from a take which had an unsatisfactory rhythm track, and married to the bass and drums from another. Thereafter, the session musicians – chosen in preference to Jimi's original sidemen because they needed to be fluent sight-readers, working from transcriptions of the original performances – filled in the gaps, bar by arduous bar.

Purists have decried the results ever since: almost all of 'Crash Landing' is music that

Jimi Hendrix never heard, at least in that form. The decision not to use Jimi's own choice of musicians to complete the recordings was universally criticised, though Douglas's excuse – that Mitch Mitchell or Billy Cox wouldn't have been experienced enough as studio players to repair odd bars or half-bars of missing music – wasn't really aired in the press at the time.

Is the album an abomination, then, from start to finish? Far from it. On purely aural evidence (i.e. without voicing an opinion on the morals of the exercise), 'Crash Landing' is a fine record, probably more enjoyable to hear than any of the posthumous studio releases apart from 'Rainbow Bridge'.

The earliest original recording on the album is 'Somewhere Over The Rainbow', which had featured the rare combination of Buddy Miles and Noel Redding back in March 1968. Their efforts were wiped and replaced, leaving Hendrix's echoed vocals surrounded by layers of guitar as he imagined the reactions of aliens looking at the planet from their swooping UFOs.

The Experience recording of 'Peace In Mississippi' from October 1968 was almost completely obliterated during the concoction of 'Crash Landing'; even one of Jimi's rhythm guitar tracks was wiped. The result was a scorching blues instrumental on which it was difficult to distinguish what was Hendrix and what was session guitarist Jeff Mironov.

The album's title track, a scathing dissection of a failing romance that incorporated some intriguing lyrics about drug use, and a vocal riff borrowed from The Beatles' 'Happiness Is A Warm Gun', was as impressive as anything on the record. It was originally taped in April 1969, as was 'Stone Free Again', a revamp of the 1966 B-side – perhaps taped when Jimi was being asked to select material for the American release of the 'Smash Hits' LP, which appeared a year after its UK counterpart. His vocal on the 'Crash Landing' reconstruction was compressed and thinned down as if it had been recorded down a phone line.

'Message To Love' and 'With The Power' (alias 'Power Of Soul') had both been included on the live 'Band Of Gypsys' album back in 1970. The studio versions received far less tinkering than anything else on the LP, and stand as perhaps the most impressive

Gypsys cuts available on record. In particular, 'Message To Love' – distressingly laboured on 'Band Of Gypsys' – finally hit Jimi's conception of a soul/rock crossover head on.

'Coming Down Hard On Me Baby', aired a year earlier on 'Loose Ends', didn't deserve its 'Crash Landing' revamp. But the final track, named 'Captain Coconut' by Alan Douglas, was a more intriguing affair – an electronic composition, no less, for electric guitar, slipping delicately through moods and movements in an almost classical vein.

It transpired that 'Captain Coconut' was not a track that Hendrix would have recognised. Based on material from tape boxes marked 'MLK' (claimed by some commentators to refer to civil rights leader Martin Luther King), it had actually been assembled from three separate groups of sessions by John Jansen, when he was creating incidental Hendrix music for the *Rainbow Bridge* movie. Eddie Kramer objected to him tampering with unconnected Hendrix fragments, but Douglas and Bongiovi accepted the piece on its undoubted musical merits, and overdubbed it accordingly. So is 'Captain Coconut' a minor Hendrix masterpiece, a per-

version of the truth, or both? Your reaction to that question is likely to determine your opinion of the entire 'Crash Landing' project.

THE CD: Musically fascinating, 'Crash Landing' might have enjoyed a better critical reception if its origins and preparation had been explained in some detailed sleevenotes. Instead, the LP – and its CD transfer – simply list the musicians on each cut, with no indication of whether their contributions were made in 1968 or 1975. Worse still, Alan Douglas awarded himself a co-writing credit for five tracks: 'Somewhere Over The Rainbow', 'Crash Landing', 'Come Down Hard On Me', 'Peace In Mississippi' and 'Captain Coconut'.

MIDNIGHT LIGHTNING

LP RELEASE: POLYDOR 2310 415 (UK), NOVEMBER 1975

CD RELEASE: POLYDOR 825 166-2 (UK), MARCH 1989

Tracks: Trashman/Midnight Lightning/Hear My Train A-Coming/Gypsy Boy (New Rising Sun)/Blue Suede Shoes/Machine Gun/Once I Had A Woman/Beginnings

THE ALBUM: Like 'Crash Landing', 'Midnight Lightning' was assembled by Alan Douglas and Tony Bongiovi. Interviewed 15 years later by *Guitar Player* magazine, Douglas admitted that the second recycling exercise had been a failure: "We were light on material, and I think I forced the issue in a couple of instances. It's just not thoroughly enjoyable, and it's not the best of Hendrix."

That's certainly true of 'Blue Suede Shoes', which was a travesty on 'Loose Ends' and wasn't rescued by the Douglas-supervised overdubs. Nor was the stripping away of Mitch Mitchell and Noel Redding's contributions to Noel's 'Midnight' (first released on 'War Heroes') a success – especially when the track was retitled 'Trashman', with the composer credit switching from Noel to Jimi.

Equally insensitive was the decision to work on another 'War Heroes' track, Mitch Mitchell's 'Beginning', and to wipe its writer's drum track from the tape. At least in the case of the clichéd blues jam, 'Once I Had A Woman' (given its title by Douglas), the raw material wasn't much to begin with.

Those disasters accounted for half of 'Midnight Lightning', but the remaining four tracks were all regular inclusions in Jimi's 1969/1970 live sets. 'Machine Gun' was the stand-out cut on 'Band Of Gypsys', for instance, but this studio rehash managed to undercut any of the song's aural drama, blurring the essence of Hendrix's anti-war lament (and a wonderful guitar solo) beneath an amateurish mix and some ill-considered session playing.

Equally ill-fated was 'Hear My Train A-Coming' (alias 'Getting My Heart Back Together Again'), usually a vehicle for some of Jimi's most passionate blues playing; and 'Gypsy Boy', a retitling of 'Hey Baby (New Rising Sun)' which bore none of the precision of the 'Rainbow Bridge' original. Finally, the album's title track epitomised the failings of the album: a pleasant, if inconsequential blues performance was buried beneath excess instrumentation and clumsy gospel vocal asides. Hendrix would have been appalled.

THE CD: No annotation, once again, very basic digital remastering, and some strange choices of titles for what should have been familiar songs.

THE ESSENTIAL JIMI HENDRIX VOLUMES ONE AND TWO

LP RELEASES: VOLUME 1, POLYDOR 2612 034 (UK),
AUGUST 1978; VOLUME 2, POLYDOR 2311 014 (UK),
JANUARY 1981
CD RELEASE: REPRISE 26035-2 (USA), NOVEMBER 1989

Tracks: Are You Experienced/Third Stone From The Sun/Purple Haze/Hey Joe/ Fire/ Foxy Lady/The Wind Cries Mary/Little Wing/If Six Was Nine/Bold As Love/Little Miss Lover/Castles Made Of Sand/Gypsy Eyes/The Burning Of The Midnight Lamp/ Voodoo Child (Slight Return)/Crosstown Traffic/Still Raining, Still Dreaming/Have You Ever Been (To Electric Ladyland)/All Along The Watch-tower/House Burning Down/ Room Full Of Mirrors/Izabella/Freedom/Dolly Dagger/Stepping Stone/Drifting/Ezy Ryder/ Wild Thing/Machine Gun/Star Spangled Banner/Gloria

THE ALBUMS: 'The Essential Jimi Hendrix' was a double-LP, Volume Two a single affair, and their obvious purpose was to present a comprehensive 'greatest hits' package to replace the outdated 'Smash Hits'. As an incentive to diehard fans, 'The Essential Jimi Hendrix' was accompanied by a one-sided

single featuring a long (but still edited) cover of Van Morrison's 'Gloria', cut during an Experience jam session at TTG Studios in October 1968. There are some obvious omissions from the two albums – notably any record of 'Red House' – but they still represent a very useful introduction to Hendrix's work.

THE CDs: The time limitations imposed by the CD format meant that one song from the original packages, Volume Two's 'I Don't Live Today', was omitted from the CD release.

NINE TO THE UNIVERSE

LP RELEASE: POLYDOR 2344 155 (UK), JUNE 1980
UNRELEASED ON OFFICIAL CD

Tracks: Nine To The Universe/Jimi-Jimmy Jam/Young-Hendrix/Easy Blues/Drone Blues
The third and (for the moment) last of Alan Douglas's 'creations' from the unissued Hendrix archives attracted a much lower profile than 'Crash Landing' or 'Midnight Lightning', and sales to match. Hendrix was scarcely a commercial force in 1980: issued five years earlier, or ten later, 'Nine To The Universe' would have been greeted as some kind of event.

For years, Douglas had been touting the musical genius of an impromptu jam session between Hendrix and jazz-rock guitarist John McLaughlin. 'Nine To The Universe' seemed like the ideal venue for this tape, but McLaughlin himself expressed his dissatisfaction with the standard of his playing, and presumably blocked the release of the album Douglas had originally intended.

Instead, the LP borrowed from a variety of Hendrix jam sessions, which to varying degrees supported Douglas's claim that Jimi was moving towards jazz in his final years. More accurate would be the acknowledgement that Hendrix loved to jam: there are countless post-1967 tapes, both live and studio, to prove it.

With the exception of the piece that gave this album its name, none of the tracks were 'songs' as such: they were selected, edited and then titled by Alan Douglas, not Hendrix. Longer versions of all five exist on bootleg tapes, incidentally.

'Jimi/Jimmy Jam' matched Hendrix with guitarist Jim McCarty (not The Yardbird but a member of the Buddy Miles Express). It was taped on March 25, 1969; almost a month

later, on April 24, Jimi and some unidentified musicians recorded the aptly titled 'Drone Blues', marked by some astounding Hendrix guitar passages.

May 14, 1969, produced the most fruitful of these jams, 'Young/Hendrix', on which Jimi was joined by Billy Cox, Buddy Miles and renowned avant-jazz organist Larry Young. For almost the only time on the record, 'Young/Hendrix' does confirm the claims of those who regard Hendrix as a pure jazz genius in the making.

Eight days later, Hendrix, Cox and Miles were back in the Record Plant studios cutting 'Message From Nine To The Universe' – in which can clearly be heard the seeds for two songs the trio would play later in the year as The Band Of Gypsys, 'Message To Love' and 'Earth Blues'.

Finally, 'Easy Blues' captured the core of the band that played Woodstock – Jimi, Larry Lee, Mitch, Juma and Billy – swinging with a lack of inhibition that would have been more usefully displayed at the festival.

'Nine To The Universe' would make a wonderful bootleg – in fact, in the absence of an official CD, it's duly become one, complete

with bonus tracks – but it is scarcely a commercial proposition, or a valid attempt to portray Hendrix as a potential jazzman. But it did attract far more favourable reviews than either of Alan Douglas's posthumous studio concoctions of the mid-70s.

THE JIMI HENDRIX CONCERTS

(VERSION 1)
LP RELEASE: CBS 88592 (UK), AUGUST 1982
CD RELEASE: MEDIA MOTION MEDIA CD 1 (UK),
AUGUST 1989

Tracks: Fire/I Don't Live Today/Red House/Stone Free/Are You Experienced/ Little Wing/Voodoo Child (Slight Return)/ Bleeding Heart/Hey Joe/Wild Thing/Hear My Train A-Comin'

THE ALBUM: Ten years after the last album of previously unissued live Hendrix performances, The Jimi Hendrix Concerts confirmed what collectors of tapes and bootlegs had known for years – that the potential seam of top-quality concert material ran deep and rich. The impact of this double-LP has been diminished in the CD age by the release of later sets like 'Live At Winterland', 'Stages' and 'Woodstock', but in 1982 it

served to provoke the revival of interest in his 'unofficial' catalogue which had effectively been smothered by the disasters of the mid-70s.

Spread across four sides, the contents made little attempt to replicate a typical Jimi Hendrix Experience performance: in fact, two of the tracks actually featured the Billy Cox/Mitch Mitchell band, rather than Mitchell and Noel Redding. But the concentration on familiar concert landmarks did hint at the intensity and power of Jimi's live work once he freed himself from the obligation to perform as a human jukebox.

The set also registered the existence of high-fidelity tapes of Hendrix's shows at the Winterland Ballroom in San Francisco during 1968. Half the album came from this venue, and although the versions of 'Fire', 'Voodoo Child (Slight Return)' and 'Wild Thing' weren't sensational, the deliciously slow 'Little Wing' was a real find. A rare performance of 'Are You Experienced', which opened with a feedback collage that would have delighted The Velvet Underground, topped even that, but Hendrix's finest playing from these Winterland extracts surfaced on an amazing 'Hear My Train A-Comin' ' – not a substantial song in Jimi's catalogue, except insofar as it liberated him to explore the depths of his blues roots.

Two songs came from the Royal Albert Hall show on February 24, 1969, inclusions which immediately reopened legal wounds created by the release of 'Experience' and 'More Experience' in the early 70s (see the Unofficial CDs section for more details). 'Bleeding Heart' was prosaic enough, but 'Stone Free' took on mammoth proportions, as Jimi soloed into the night, almost regardless of what song he was playing, before Mitch Mitchell replied in kind. Jimi responded with a gentle flamenco passage, easing The Experience back into a chorus that had long since become irrelevant.

The remaining three tracks sampled one song apiece from San Diego in May 1969 ('I Don't Live Today', as reissued later on 'Stages'); Berkeley in May 1970 (a scrappy 'Hey Joe'); and Randall's Island in July 1970 (a surprisingly short eight minutes of 'Red House', with a characteristically emotional solo).

THE CD: Problems with the then fledging science of CD mastering forced Media Motion Media to snip vital seconds from the original running order, by omitting Hendrix's spoken introductions from the disc. As on the original LP cover, 'Little Wing' and 'Fire' were misdated by two days, while Elmore James' 'Bleeding Heart' was credited one more time to Hendrix himself.

THE JIMI HENDRIX CONCERTS
(VERSION 2)
CD RELEASE: CASTLE CCSCD 235 (UK), FEBRUARY 1990

Tracks: Fire/I Don't Live Today/Red House/Stone Free/Are You Experienced/ Little Wing/Voodoo Child (Slight Return)/ Bleeding Heart/Hey Joe/Wild Thing/Getting My Heart Back Together Again/Foxy Lady

No sooner was the Media Motion Media edition of this album in the shops than its status was being questioned. To avoid possible legal complications, the album was licensed by the Jimi Hendrix Estate, in the person of Alan Douglas, to Castle Communications. Their edition added one song to the original track listing – a wonderfully frenetic 'Foxey (sic) Lady' from the LA Forum on April 26, 1969.

THE SINGLES ALBUM

LP RELEASE: POLYDOR PODV 6 (UK), FEBRUARY 1983
CD RELEASE: POLYDOR 827 369-2 (GERMANY),
APRIL 1986

*Tracks: Hey Joe/Stone Free/Purple Haze/
51st Anniversary/The Wind Cries Mary/
Highway Chile/The Burning Of The Midnight
Lamp/The Stars That Play With Laughing
Sam's Dice/All Along The Watchtower/Long
Hot Summer Night/Crosstown Traffic/ Fire/
Voodoo Child (Slight Return)/Angel/ Night
Bird Flying/Gypsy Eyes/Remember/Johnny B.
Goode/Little Wing/Foxy Lady/Manic
Depression/Third Stone From The Sun/Gloria*
THE ALBUM: Self-explanatory in theory, this
set was intended to include every song issued
on a UK Hendrix 45rpm single, before and
after his death. It didn't quite achieve its aim –
it missed the coupling of the acoustic 'Hear
My Train A Comin' and the Monterey 'Rock
Me Baby', released in a vain attempt of cash-
ing in on the Jimi Hendrix film soundtrack LP
in 1973 – but otherwise this remains a useful
place to find all the original A- and B-sides
from the Sixties, plus 'Gloria' from The
Essential Jimi Hendrix.

Polydor filled out the set with some non-
single tracks, like 'Manic Depression' and
'Third Stone From The Sun': fans would no
doubt rather have had the original single mixes
of the US Band Of Gypsys single, 'Stepping
Stone'/'Izabella'.

Note that two tracks, 'Johnny B. Goode'
and 'Little Wing', are live recordings originally
issued on Hendrix In The West.

KISS THE SKY

LP RELEASE: POLYDOR 823 704-1 (UK), NOVEMBER 1984
CD RELEASE: POLYDOR 823 704-2 (UK),
NOVEMBER 1984

*Tracks: Are You Experienced/I Don't Live
Today/Voodoo Child (Slight Return)/Stepping
Stone/Castles Made Of Sand/Killing Floor/
Purple Haze/Red House/Crosstown Traffic/
Third Stone From The Sun/All Along The
Watchtower*
THE ALBUM: 'Kiss The Sky' was an Alan
Douglas creation designed as a Jimi Hendrix
primer, which concentrated on the sonic ebul-
lience of his guitar playing, rather than hit sin-
gles. Collectors lapped up the few seconds of
studio chatter added to the take of 'Red
House' originally issued on the US 'Smash
Hits' LP, and the presence of a slightly

remixed 'Stepping Stone' from the 1969 Band Of Gypsys single. Otherwise this was familiar material all the way – with 'Killin' Floor' pulled from the Monterey performance, and 'I Don't Live Today' from the San Diego Sports Arena, as heard first on 'The Jimi Hendrix Concerts'.

THE CD: This was the first Hendrix CD to be issued simultaneously with the vinyl edition.

JOHNNY B. GOODE

LP RELEASE: FAME FA 3160 (UK), JULY 1986
CD RELEASE: CAPITOL 432018-2 (USA), 1990

Tracks: Voodoo Chile/All Along The Watchtower/Star Spangled Banner/Johnny B. Goode/Machine Gun

THE ALBUM: Years after Hendrix's death, the legal battles that he inadvertently initiated were still rumbling through the courts. The appearance of this album on EMI-owned labels – Fame in Britain, Capitol in the States – was presumably the result of some settlement of the case between Jimi, his management and Ed Chalpin, producer of the Curtis Knight sessions (see the final section of this book for more information).

Chalpin signed over his rights to release the 'Band Of Gypsys' LP to Capitol in the States, and the same agreement presumably entitled the label to release this half-hearted 'mini-LP' sixteen years later.

Designed as the soundtrack to an equally brief home-video release, it repeated the remarkable 'Johnny B. Goode' from 'Hendrix In The West', added 'Machine Gun' from the same Berkeley show in May 1970, and filled out the set with three ragged performances from Atlanta in July 1970. The 'Star Spangled Banner' from this show is a smirk compared to the agonised wail of the Woodstock rendition. Alan Douglas evidently thought so little of the 'All Along The Watchtower' from Atlanta, though, that he didn't bother to include it when devoting an entire CD to the concert in the 'Stages' box set.

THE CD: The liner notes wrongly suggest that all five of these performances can be seen in the 'Johnny B. Goode' video; 'Machine Gun' can't.

JIMI PLAYS MONTEREY

POLYDOR 827 990-2 (UK), SEPTEMBER 1986
REPRISE 9 25358-2 (US), SEPTEMBER 1986

Tracks: Killing Floor/Foxy Lady/Like A Rolling Stone/Rock Me Baby/Hey Joe/Can You See Me/The Wind Cries Mary/Purple Haze/Wild Thing

Nineteen years after The Jimi Hendrix Experience made their début American performance, those who weren't at the Monterey showgrounds in June 1967 were finally able to see (almost) their full show, when DA Pennebaker's Jimi Plays Monterey was unveiled at the Toronto International Film Festival on September 7, 1986.

To coincide with that première, Polydor released this CD, which gave an official release to a set that had been circulating via a mix of official and bootleg recordings for years. The Monterey Pop film from the late Sixties had included snippets of Jimi's set; then a 1970 LP, issued the week Hendrix died, combined five of his Monterey songs with as many from another ill-fated star, Otis Redding.

While Pennebaker's cameras missed a song or two from The Experience's 40 min-utes on stage, the audio tapes captured the entire drama. Hendrix arrived back in America as an unknown; he quit the Monterey stage an international star. The festival crowd had just seen The Who destroy their equipment in a bout of amphetamine-fuelled exhibitionism; now they watched mouths agape as Hendrix unveiled all the crowd-pleasing tracks he'd picked up during his years on the club and bar circuit.

His Monterey set opened with a crushing 'Killing Floor', fully in keeping with the contemporary rock vogue for revamped R&B standards. 'Foxy Lady' established his credentials as a flirt, before Jimi risked everything by daring to cover Bob Dylan's 'Like A Rolling Stone' – as close to a sacred object as anything in the world of 1967 rock. His reading, simultaneously cocky and restrained, was little short of a masterpiece, and after that he was home and dry.

'Rock Me Baby', a slightly nervous 'Hey Joe' and 'Can You See Me' were punctuated with Jimi's near-embarrassing stage patter – a curious mix of naïvety and utter coolness. 'The Wind Cries Mary' and 'Purple Haze' illustrated the extremes of his artistic reach, before Jimi announced: "I'm gonna sacrifice something that I really love. Don't think I'm silly, 'cos I don't think that I'm losing my mind." No-one in the audience could have been prepared for what followed, as Hendrix performed 'Wild Thing' – starting out with the movements of a burlesque dancer, and then metamorphosing into a shaman or a madman as he ignited his guitar, and seemed to cast spells over the audience as it burned. Roadies raced on stage to salvage the house PA; the star-packed audience howled their approval and disbelief. For once, the old clichés of overnight success were justified – and the entire episode is captured intact on the American edition of 'Jimi Plays Monterey', which retains more of the stage atmosphere and announcements than the European CD.

THE BEST OF JIMI HENDRIX

EMI CDP 746 485 2 (EUROPE), MAY 1987

Tracks: Who Knows/Machine Gun/Hear My Train A-Comin'/Foxy Lady/Power To Love/ Message Of Love/Voodoo Chile/Stone Free/Ezy Ryder

Even the major labels can't be trusted, it seems. The 'best' of Hendrix in this case was actually a mix of tracks from the original 'Band Of Gypsys' album ('Who Knows', 'Machine Gun', 'Power Of Love' and 'Message Of Love'), and from 'Band Of Gypsys 2' – the misbegotten US vinyl LP issued in 1986. As with the original album, 'Voodoo Child (Slight Return)', 'Stone Free' and 'Ezy Ryder' weren't Band Of Gypsys performances, but live cuts from Atlanta and Berkeley in 1970.

LIVE AT WINTERLAND

POLYDOR 833 004-2 (UK), 1988

Tracks: Prologue/Fire/Manic Depression/ The Sunshine Of Your Love/Spanish Castle Magic/Red House/Killing Floor/Tax Free/ Foxy Lady/Hey Joe/Purple Haze/Wild Thing/Epilogue

THE ALBUM: Over three nights and six shows at the Winterland Ballroom in San Francisco, Jimi Hendrix, Noel Redding and Mitch Mitchell created some of the most magnificent, and sometimes unfocused, music of their joint career. The concerts ran twice nightly on October 10-12, 1968, coinciding with the release of 'Electric Ladyland',

and the same sense of expansion and ambition that soaked the studio record also infused the live shows. But even allowing for a cameo appearance by Jefferson Airplane's Jack Casady on bass for one show, Hendrix didn't have the musical support or the studio overdubbing facilities to reproduce the sonic voyages of 'Ladyland' on stage. Instead, he and his rhythm section explored the dynamics of the power trio – wavering dangerously close to the line between extravagance and excess which their rivals, Cream, crossed more often than not in 1968.

No songs were picked from the first show of the season, but the second allowed Casady to pummel his rib-bending bass-lines in time-honoured style on a chaotic but dutifully intense 'Killin' Floor', while the three-piece butchered (appropriately enough) Cream's 'Sunshine Of Your Love' as a gesture to Clapton, Baker and Bruce's recent decision to disband.

By contrast, the first show from the next night, October 11, provided a magnificent 'Red House' – slow, majestic, precise. At the second house, Hendrix treated 'Fire' like a plaything, letting the guitar speak the chorus as the rhythm duo struggled to keep pace. 'Tax Free' (see 'War Heroes' for the story of that song) veered between genius and disaster, while Hendrix turned 'Foxy Lady' into a joyous feeding frenzy of feedback. It was obviously a wild night.

A long triple-play was taken from the first show on the 12th – Hendrix pumping his guitar into cacophony before lurching into 'Hey Joe', then 'Purple Haze' and finally 'Wild Thing'. The last gig of the residency added a fine 'Manic Depression', and an equally inspired 'Spanish Castle Magic'. The overall result? A narrow but thrilling victory for artistic nerve over sheer exuberance.

THE CD: 'Spanish Castle Magic' and 'Foxy Lady' both exposed the limitations of the original tape source: there again, who wanted pure digital sound from Hendrix in '68? Note that Rykodisc prepared a 'gold disc' CD edition of 'Live At Winterland' for the US market, supposedly guaranteeing even better sound.

P.S. Wonder if Alan Douglas secured copyright clearance for the few seconds of Procol Harum's 'A Whiter Shade Of Pale' which introduce this CD?

LIVE AT WINTERLAND + 3
RYKODISC RCD 20038+3 (USA), SEPTEMBER 1992

Tracks: full contents of above 'Live At Winterland' release, plus bonus tracks on CD single: Are You Experienced/Voodoo Child (Slight Return)/Like A Rolling Stone

If the cash-crazy exploiters of the Nineties had been let loose on the Sixties, what fun they could have had. Let me see: how about two different editions of 'Electric Ladyland', one with the long 'Voodoo Chile', the other with 'Voodoo Child (Slight Return)', so that true fans would have to buy both?

Some of that entirely self-serving marketing spirit was exhibited nakedly when Rykodisc, who'd issued the original 'Live At Winterland' in the States, prepared a special commemorative edition of the CD four years later. Inside a box with the CD was a T-shirt (whoopee) and a three-track CD single, featuring performances that weren't available anywhere else. Even allowing for the fact that the three songs ran to 30 minutes – 12 of 'Like A Rolling Stone', 14 of 'Are You Experienced – this was a particularly shabby trick, especially when the entire package retailed for $40. All the new tracks were tak-

en from October 11, two from the first show, 'Like A Rolling Stone' from the second.

RADIO ONE (VERSION 1)
CASTLE CCSCD 212 (UK), FEBRUARY 1989

Tracks: Stone Free/Radio One/Day Tripper/ Killin' Floor/Love Or Confusion/ Drivin' South/Catfish Blues/Wait Until Tomorrow/ Getting My Heart Back Together Again/ Hound Dog/ Fire/I'm Your Hoochie Coochie Man/Purple Haze/Spanish Castle Magic/Hey Joe/Foxy Lady/The Burning Of The Midnight Lamp

THE ALBUM: Between January 30, 1966, and December 15, 1967, The Jimi Hendrix Experience recorded eight exclusive sessions for BBC Radio. Though these quickfire recordings represent a fascinating insight into the band's development that year, they weren't made for artistic or historic reasons. Instead, the Hendrix sessions, and thousands like them by artists major and minor, were required by the BBC to fill their airtime, as an agreement with the Musicians' Union prevented the organisation from filling their shows with records: a certain percentage of the music which went out over the British airwaves had to be recorded specifically for the BBC, in theory as entirely live performances (though the rules were bent to allow the minimum of overdubbing).

More than two decades after these tapes were made – and eighteen years after unofficial recordings of the shows began to circulate on bootlegs – the Hendrix Estate, via Alan Douglas, finally prepared a fully legal and (almost) accurately documented record of Jimi's encounters with the BBC. 'Radio One' featured 17 tracks, while an additional two were available on tie-in releases (see below). The track selection wasn't entirely uncontroversial, as many diehards wanted to see Hendrix's cover of Bob Dylan's 'Can You Please Crawl Out Your Window' preserved for posterity, but what was included was still more than sufficient to attract copious critical plaudits.

Much of 'Radio One' simply transferred The Experience's regular live repertoire into the studio, where they had the benefits of equipment that would function correctly but lost the stimulus of an audience. But the album also highlighted those occasions on which Hendrix surmounted the dry atmosphere of the BBC

studios, and created moments of genius. The collaboration with British blues veteran Alexis Korner on Willie Dixon's 'I'm Your Hoochie Coochie Man' was particularly momentous, as Korner's slide guitar fills incited Jimi to some spectacular guitar breaks of his own. Equally majestic was 'Catfish Blues' – like the Korner session, taped in October 1967 – and a remarkable 'Hear My Train A-Comin' ', from December, on which The Experience were inspired into some magnificent blues playing by an in-house bunch of revellers.

But the performance which on its own justified all the hype for 'Radio One' was an instrumental, 'Drivin' South'. Jimi had worked up the song during his days with Curtis Knight and The Squires, but by December 1967 it had become a vehicle for a breathtaking barrage of chords and flailing lead lines, surpassed for excitement and dexterity in Jimi's catalogue only by the 'Voodoo Child (Slight Return)' that closed the 'Electric Ladyland' album the following year.

THE CD: The flat ambience of the BBC studios worked its usual dampening act even on The Jimi Hendrix Experience, giving these recordings a thinner sound than his other

1967 output. That problem aside, the presentation of Radio One was commendable – though two tracks were slightly miscredited (see below), and the sleeve-notes repeated the 15-year-old myth that John Lennon had been in the studio to assist The Experience with their rather scrappy cover of The Beatles' 'Day Tripper'. Incidentally, Rykodisc in the States, who issued this set just before Castle in Britain, also prepared a picture CD edition.

RADIO ONE (VERSION 2)
VICTOR VDP 1454 (JAPAN) C. 1990

Tracks: Stone Free/Radio One/Day Tripper/Killin' Floor/Love Or Confusion/ Drivin' South/Catfish Blues/Wait Until Tomorrow/Getting My Heart Back Together Again/Hound Dog/Fire/I'm Your Hoochie Coochie Man/Purple Haze/Spanish Castle Magic/Hey Joe/Foxy Lady/The Burning Of The Midnight Lamp/Hear My Train A-Comin'/Drivin' South

The Japanese release of the BBC sessions added the two final tracks, both issued originally on the US 'Day Tripper' CD single. Though Rykodisc claimed that they had never

been broadcast at the time, it was actually the versions of these songs included on the original 'Radio One' line-up which were being unveiled for the first time.

LIVE AND UNRELEASED
CASTLE HBCD 100 (UK), NOVEMBER 1989

Tracks (* means track is incomplete; all 3 CDs also include interviews)
CD1: Purple Haze*/I Don't Live Today*/ Remember*/Stone Free*/Cherokee Mist*/ Star Spangled Banner*/Bleeding Heart*/ Testify Part 1*/Driving South*/I'm A Man*/ Like A Rolling Stone*/Little One*/Red House*/Hey Joe/Instrumental*/I'm Your Hoochie Coochie Man*/Purple Haze/ Instrumental*/The Wind Cries Mary/Love Or Confusion*/Foxy Lady
CD2: Third Stone From The Sun*/Killing Floor*/Wild Thing/Tax Free*/May This Be Love*/Mr Bad Luck/The Burning Of The Midnight Lamp*/The Burning Of The Midnight Lamp/You've Got Me Floating*/Spanish Castle Magic/Bold As Love/One Rainy Wish/Little Wing/Driving South/The Things I Used To Do*/All Along The Watchtower/ Drifter's Escape/Cherokee Mist*/Voodoo

Chile*/Voodoo Child (Slight Return)/. . . And
The Gods Made Love*/1983 . . . (A Merman I
Should Turn To Be)*
CD3: Have You Ever Been (To Electric
Ladyland)*/Voodoo Chile*/Voodoo Chile*/
Rainy Day, Dream Away*/Come On (Part
1)/Fire*/Manic Depression/Astro Man*/The
Stars That Play With Laughing Sam's Dice*/
Machine Gun*/Stepping Stone*/Room Full Of
Mirrors/Angel/Rainy Day Shuffle*/Valleys Of
Neptune*/Drifting*/Send My Love To Linda/
Send My Love To Linda*/South Saturn
Delta*/God Save The Queen*/Dolly Dagger/
Can I Whisper In Your Ear*/Night Bird Flying/
Getting My Heart Back Together Again*
THE ALBUMS: Over Labor Day weekend in
1988, the US radio syndication network
Westwood One made available for broadcast
an afternoon-long special entitled Jimi Hendrix:
Live And Unreleased. It comprised a four-hour
(with commercials) documentary of Jimi's life
and career, and a further hour devoted to the
broadcast of The Experience's LA Forum concert from April 26, 1969.

To distant British fans, the entire exercise
was frustratingly tantalising – the prospect of
hours of unissued Hendrix material being
weighed against the solely US distribution of
Westwood One's product. The release of this
three-CD set brought everyone back down to
earth. With the commercials stripped away,
the documentary section of the show now
stretched for a little over three hours.
Meanwhile, the LA Forum show wasn't
licensed for official UK release.

Worse still, the format of the show was
designed to appeal to American audiences,
not British. If the BBC had broadcast the epic,
then they would no doubt have aired a suc-
cession of rare recordings, introducing each
one with relevant information and then leaving
the music to be heard without interruptions. In
the States, the unissued tracks were stitched
into a music/words tapestry that often meant
that collectors were reduced to straining their
ears to catch a few seconds of previously
unheard guitar wizardry beneath the banal
narration.

Interviews with Pete Townshend, Mick
Jagger, Mitch Mitchell, Chas Chandler and
Hendrix himself accompanied the music, creating a show that was highly enjoyable listening
on its first play, but quickly palled thereafter. A
large proportion of the musical content was

less "Live And Unreleased" than over-familiar, and almost all of the unreleased tracks were presented in incomplete, sometimes fragmentary form.

For all that, the set did allow us our first legal exposure to minor gems like Jimi's solo demos of 'Angel', 'Voodoo Child (Slight Return)' and 'Cherokee Mist'; the jazzy, experimental textures of the instrumental 'South Saturn Delta', from June 1968; a wonderful 1967 studio take of 'Look Over Yonder', preceding the Rainbow Bridge cut by a year; and a radical remix of '1983' from the 'Electric Ladyland' album. Also included, though, were Sting performing 'Little Wing' (legal problems forced Castle to withdraw the set because Sting hadn't given his permission), and several Little Richard tracks which were supposed to, but didn't, feature Hendrix on guitar. A mixed, often infuriating bag, to be sure.

THE CDs: The CD booklet, the back cover of the set, and the actual encoding of the CDs themselves all give different information about the number of tracks on each disc. Large segments of the show are grouped together as one 'track', making it impossible to cue up a particular performance on any of the CDs.

Equally annoying are the many errors in the skimpy booklet, which claims, for example, that Jimi worked with Curtis Knight in 1964, not 1965.

ARE YOU EXPERIENCED/ BAND OF GYPSYS/ HENDRIX IN THE WEST/ WAR HEROES

POLYDOR 839 875-2 (UK), 1989

Tracks: as original CDs

This pointless box set collected a seemingly random collection of Hendrix LPs, in their most primitive state of CD remastering, and added them to a skimpy booklet. Worth investigating only if you can't find the individual releases of 'Hendrix In The West' and 'War Heroes'.

THE JIMI HENDRIX REFERENCE SERIES

FUZZ, FEEDBACK & WAH-WAH

HAL LEONARD HL00660036 (USA), 1989

Tracks (all extracts): Drivin' South/Drivin' South/Freedom/Peace In Mississippi/Purple Haze/Manic Depression/Love Or Confusion/

Bold As Love/Spanish Castle Magic/Spanish Castle Magic/If Six Was Nine/Little Miss Lover/Stone Free/Foxy Lady/Foxy Lady/Third Stone From The Sun/EXP/Wild Thing/Look Over Yonder/Ezy Ryder/Red House/Stone Free/Are You Experienced/The Burning Of The Midnight Lamp/Up From The Skies/Up From The Skies/Little Miss Lover/Voodoo Child (Slight Return)/Still Raining, Still Dreaming/Belly Button Window/Tax Free/Changes/Who Knows/Are You Experienced/Straight Ahead/In From The Storm/Red House/Red House/Red House/Message To Love/Tax Free/1983 . . . (A Merman I Should Turn To Be)

WHAMMY BAR & FINGER GREASE
HAL LEONARD HL00660038 (USA), 1989
REPACKAGED AS HL00660279 IN 1992

Tracks (all extracts): Star Spangled Banner/Third Stone From The Sun/Machine Gun/Star Spangled Banner/Pali Gap/Look Over Yonder/I Don't Live Today/Tax Free/Cherokee Mist/Star Spangled Banner/Machine Gun/Machine Gun/Ain't No Telling/Machine Gun/Machine Gun/House Burning Down/Hey Joe/Red House/Foxy

Lady/Astro Man/Drivin' South/Machine Gun/Spanish Castle Magic/Manic Depression/Bold As Love/Third Stone From The Sun/Third Stone From The Sun/Astro Man/Drivin' South/Machine Gun/God Save The Queen/Spanish Castle Magic/Machine Gun/The Wind Cries Mary/May This Be Love/Third Stone From The Sun/Astro Man/Star Spangled Banner/Spanish Castle Magic

RED HOUSE: VARIATIONS ON A THEME
HAL LEONARD HL00660040 (USA), 1989
REPACKAGED IN 1992 AS HL00699358

Tracks: six versions of Red House by Hendrix, plus Red House by John Lee Hooker

OCTAVIA & UNIVIBE
HAL LEONARD HL00660275 (USA), 1993

Tracks (all extracts): Purple Haze/Fire/One Rainy Wish/Little Miss Lover/Tax Free/MLK/Angel/Little Wing/Dolly Dagger/Pali Gap/Star Spangled Banner/Night Bird Flying/Drifting/Astro Man/Instrumental Solo/In From The Storm/Star Spangled Banner/Dolly Dagger/Machine Gun/Little Wing/Machine Gun/Midnight/Voodoo Child

(Slight Return)/Hey Baby (The Land Of The New Rising Sun)/Who Knows

RHYTHM

HAL LEONARD HL00660281 (USA), 1993

Tracks (all extracts): Killing Floor/Killing Floor/Stone Free/Stone Free/Manic Depression/Love Or Confusion/Love Or Confusion/Wait Until Tomorrow/Ain't No Telling/Fire/Driving South/You've Got Me Floating/Bold As Love/Little Wing/Little Wing/Castles Made Of Sand/Electric Lady Land/Voodoo Child (Slight Return)/Jam 292/Still Raining, Still Dreaming/Come On (Part 1)/Stone Free/Freedom/Johnny B. Goode/Jam H290/Gypsy Eyes/Message To Love/Message To Love/Lover Man/Bleeding Heart/ Beginning/ Midnight/ Spanish Castle Magic

This series of five instructional packages comprises 'The Jimi Hendrix Reference Series', a combination of printed music and aural evidence whose aim, according to Alan Douglas, is "rooting Jimi in the academic arena, and analysing every aspect of the guitar defined by Jimi Hendrix". With the exception of the Red House volume, the

'Reference Series' is aimed at sight-reading guitar players rather than casual listeners: the CDs or cassettes in each package are fully annotated on music sheets, together with explanations of how, to quote former Wings guitarist Laurence Juber (a consultant for the project), Jimi "unlocked the potential of noise for music-making by learning how to control its power by subtle techniques".

All five of the CDs contain otherwise unavailable material, but all but one of them – Red House is the exception again – divides Jimi's work into fragments illustrating a particular technique or trademark. Approached without scholarly intentions, the CDs form strange collages of sound, offering frustratingly brief extracts from solos and riffs, like a 'name that tune' quiz without a question-master.

'Fuzz, Feedback & Wah-Wah' and 'Rhythm' cover self-explanatory ground, but the subject of 'Whammy Bar & Fingergrease' needs further explication: 'whammy bar' is the name given to the guitar's vibrato (tremolo) arm, which stretches the string and alters its pitch; 'finger grease' is a catch-all description for Jimi's unique approach to the instrument. Amusingly, this CD includes one brief performance ('God Save The Queen') which isn't by Jimi but by a soundalike.

'Octavia & Univibe' are two electronic devices which Hendrix utilised during the second half of his recording career. The Octavia was a Roger Mayer invention, which doubled the note that Jimi was playing, at the same pitch but an octave higher; while the Univibe, a device first used at Woodstock, produced a quavering guitar sound similar to that you'd get from playing the instrument through a Leslie speaker.

That leaves the most enticing of these five CDs, 'Red House: Variations On A Theme'. Originally, this was meant to feature eight complete renditions of Jimi's blues classic, but restrictions of space limited the contents to six, plus a redundant, coals-to-Newcastle cover by R&B veteran John Lee Hooker, which might more usefully have been replaced by one of Jimi's original studio takes of the song.

The six performances on the CD are as follows: Winterland, October 10, 1968; TTG Studios, October 29, 1968 (also now available on the ':Blues' CD, but listed here as dating from 1969); Royal Albert Hall, February 24, 1969; LA Forum, April 26, 1969 (also available on the US box set 'Lifelines'); Berkeley, May 30, 1970; and Randall's Island, July 17, 1970 (first released on 'The Jimi Hendrix Concerts', but listed here as coming from the Newport Pop Festival, June 20, 1969).

According to *Guitar Player* editor Tom Wheeler, "It's a collection that demonstrates that if Jimi Hendrix had confined himself solely to conventional blues structures and ignored the other realms in which he was so creative, so dominant, he still could have established himself as one of the electric guitar's towering practitioners." The same contention later inspired the compilation of the ':Blues' CD, which remains easier to enjoy, and track down.

CORNERSTONES 1967-1970
POLYDOR 847 231-2 (UK), OCTOBER 1990

Tracks: Hey Joe/Purple Haze/The Wind Cries Mary/Foxy Lady/Crosstown Traffic/All Along The Watchtower/Voodoo Child (Slight Return)/Have You Ever Been To (Electric Ladyland)/Star Spangled Banner/Stepping Stone/Room Full Of Mirrors/Ezy Ryder/

Freedom/Drifting/In From The Storm/ Angel/ Fire/Stone Free

THE ALBUM: This rather pointless compilation was assembled by UK Polydor to capitalise on the hype which marked the 20th anniversary of Jimi's death. Besides the early singles, its choice of material was rather erratic, and the decision to end the set with two previously unissued tracks, 'Fire' and 'Stone Free' from Atlanta, on July 4, 1970, provoked some cynicism – particularly when neither of them was included on the 'Stages' box set, which included a less-than-full CD devoted to this show. 'Cornerstones' was withdrawn a couple of years later, and replaced by 'The Ultimate Experience'.

THE CD: The sound quality was reasonable enough, but the package was as sloppy as fans had come to expect from UK-originated projects – photos printed back to front, erroneous information, etc. Particularly baffling was the notion that Jimi and Billy Cox had first performed together "while they were in the Army in 1981"...

LIFELINES

REPRISE 9 26435-2 (USA), NOVEMBER 1990

Tracks (* means track is incomplete; CDs 1-3 also include interviews):

CD1: Purple Haze*/I Don't Live Today*/ Remember*/Stone Free*/Cherokee Mist*/ Star Spangled Banner*/Bleeding Heart*/ Testify Part 1*/Driving South*/I'm A Man*/ Like A Rolling Stone*/51st Anniversary*/ Little One*/Red House/Hey Joe/ Instrumental*/I'm Your Hoochie Coochie Man*/Purple Haze/Instrumental*/The Wind Cries Mary/ Love Or Confusion*/Foxy Lady

CD2: Are You Experienced*/Third Stone From The Sun*/Killing Floor*/Wild Thing*/ Rock Me, Baby*/Tax Free*/May This Be Love*/Mr Bad Luck/The Burning Of The Midnight Lamp*/The Burning Of The Midnight Lamp/You've Got Me Floating*/Spanish Castle Magic/Bold As Love/One Rainy Wish/Little Wing*/Little Wing/Driving South/The Things I Used To Do*/Can You Please Crawl Out Your Window*/All Along The Watchtower/All Along The Watchtower*/Like A Rolling Stone*/Drifter's Escape*/ Cherokee Mist*/Voodoo Chile*/Voodoo Child (Slight Return)/. . . And The Gods Made

Love*/1983 . . . (A Merman I Should Turn To Be)
CD3: Have You Ever Been (To Electric Ladyland)*/Voodoo Chile*/Rainy Day, Dream Away*/Come On (Part 1)/Fire*/Manic Depression/Astro Man*/The Stars That Play With Laughing Sam's Dice*/Machine Gun*/Stepping Stone*/Room Full Of Mirrors/Angel/Rainy Day Shuffle*/Valleys Of Neptune*/Drifting*/Send My Love To Linda/Send My Love To Linda*/South Saturn Delta*/God Save The Queen*/Dolly Dagger/ Can I Whisper In Your Ear*/Night Bird Flying/Getting My Heart Back Together Again*
CD4: Tax Free/Red House/Spanish Castle Magic/Star Spangled Banner/Purple Haze/I Don't Live Today/Voodoo Child (Slight Return)/The Sunshine Of Your Love

The 'Live And Unreleased' set unveiled in Britain during 1989 wasn't issued in the States. Instead, an expanded version appeared in America a year later. It fundamentally repeated the contents of the UK set, merely tinkering a little with the track listing and wherever possible upgrading the sound quality of the rare recordings. "We

found better sources for some of the tracks we used on the original radio show," explained engineer Bruce Gary, "and upgraded them accordingly for this new set. We found a stereo version of 'Angel', we've expanded the 'Red House' track from the Paris concert, and we have a better version of the '1983' demo track."

'Lifelines' won more kudos from fans for restoring the April 26, 1969, LA Forum show which had filled the final hour of the original Westwood One radio special in 1988. Sadly, though, this CD didn't contain the entire performance, as Gary attempted to explain: "'Foxy Lady' just didn't fit timewise on the CD, and since it's already available on the 'Jimi Hendrix Concerts' package, we decided to omit it." At least that had some logic behind it, unlike the decision to mix out some of Hendrix's vocals on the LA performance of 'Voodoo Child (Slight Return)'.

SESSIONS
POLYDOR 847 232-2 (UK), FEBRUARY 1991
Comprises US CDs of Are You Experienced/ Electric Ladyland/The Cry Of Love/Axis: Bold As Love

The box itself was attractive enough, but otherwise this four-CD set was simply repackaging, and unnecessary repackaging at that. Included were the revamped US versions of the first four Hendrix studio albums, three okayed by him, 'The Cry Of Love' completed after his death. 'Are You Experienced' is therefore not the original UK track listing, despite the fact that this set was prepared for British release.

Accompanying the box was a brief, rather ugly booklet, with sleeve-notes by one John Tracy – who describes, quite humourlessly, the act of 'Electric Ladyland' charting in America as "beneath the Star-Spangled Banner 6307 galloped into her equivalent tabulations", and then adds "precious yellow metal was claimed on November 19th". 'Gold disc' was presumably too simple a construction for Mr Tracy to manage.

FOOTLIGHTS
POLYDOR 847 235-2 (UK), FEBRUARY 1991

Comprises new Isle Of Wight & Band Of Gypsys CDs, plus Live At Winterland & Jimi Plays Monterey

Footlights was another UK operation, unveiling the 'new' versions of the 'Band Of Gypsys' and 'Isle Of Wight' CDs in Britain for the first time. Thankfully, they were both available separately, which prevented fans from having to duplicate their previous purchases of the Winterland and Monterey sets.

LIVE ISLE OF WIGHT '70
POLYDOR 847 236-2 (UK), JUNE 1991

Tracks: Intro/God Save The Queen/ Message To Love/Voodoo Chile/Lover Man/Machine Gun/Dolly Dagger/Red House/In From The Storm/New Rising Sun

"I have a problem with the whole set," explained Alan Douglas when he was quizzed about his plans for the Isle Of Wight tapes. "With a film, it's OK. As a record, there's no new interesting tracks on it." But 1991 still saw the release of a home-video and a live CD, both documenting a performance that Eddie Kramer described as "awful", and Hendrix himself regarded with some degree of anguish, as the video makes clear. As a psychodrama, the Isle Of Wight show is compelling viewing – Jimi never quite connected with the spiritual centre of his music, and his face reflected self-disgust allied with frustration as each attempt to bend the cacophonous noise of his guitar into structured sound collapsed into failure. Hendrix ended the show by tossing his instrument to the ground in a mixture of contempt and despair.

Much of that confusion is captured on the 'official' CD record of the show, which replaced the strictly UK-only 'Isle Of Wight' album issued in 1971. 'Message To Love' features a guitar solo that wanders plaintively into a different key from the one that Billy Cox is playing in; even the ever-reliable Mitch Mitchell seems to be thrashing his kit as much in desperation as for any definite purpose.

Alan Douglas's track selection doesn't always do Jimi too many favours, omitting (for example) by far the strongest track on 'Isle Of Wight', 'Freedom', but retaining the lacklustre opening salvo of 'God Save The Queen'. As usual, the running order of the original show was abandoned in favour of a more listenable revamp. For similar reasons, Mitch Mitchell's drum solo was edited out of the majestic 'In From The Storm', one of the few survivors from the first CD of the show. Left in, though, were Jimi's telltale between-song intros,

which clearly reveal his dissatisfaction with the sound, his guitar, his state of mind and the audience; and the accidental walkie-talkie chatter picked up over the PA during 'Machine Gun', which is exactly what was pissing Jimi off.

STAGES

POLYDOR 511 763-2 (UK), FEBRUARY 1992

Tracks:

CD1: Sgt. Pepper's Lonely Hearts Club Band/Fire/The Wind Cries Mary/Foxy Lady/ Hey Joe/I Don't Live Today/The Burning Of The Midnight Lamp/Purple Haze

CD2: Killing Floor/Catfish Blues/Foxy Lady/ Red House/Driving South/Tune-Up Song (Spanish Castle Magic)/The Wind Cries Mary/Fire/Little Wing/Purple Haze

CD3: Fire/Hey Joe/Spanish Castle Magic/ Red House/I Don't Live Today/Purple Haze/ Voodoo Child (Slight Return)

CD4: Fire/Lover Man/Spanish Castle Magic/Foxy Lady/Purple Haze/Getting My Heart Back Together Again/Stone Free/Star Spangled Banner/Straight Ahead/Room Full Of Mirrors/Voodoo Child (Slight Return)

THE ALBUMS: Twenty-one years after Jimi Hendrix's death, the treatment of his back catalogue had become more controversial than at any time since the mid-70s. The fans demanded completeness – undubbed, unedited studio out-takes, and full-length live shows. The Estate, through the mouthpiece of Alan Douglas's Are You Experienced Ltd., were still attempting to remake Hendrix in their own image.

In that dispute, Stages was a definite compromise from Douglas. Though it's by no means perfect, hardly any of the posthumous Jimi releases have been greeted with such unanimous delight by fans and collectors alike.

The theory was simple enough: to present four complete Hendrix shows, one from each year from 1967 to 1970. 1967 was represented by The Experience (Jimi, Noel and Mitch) in Studio 4 of Stockholm's Radiohuset, for a live broadcast on September 5, that year. For 1968, Douglas dug up the much-bootlegged tapes of The Experience at the Paris Olympia four months later – on January 29, to be exact.

The 1969 show was from San Diego Sports Arena on May 24, with The Experience at one of their final shows. Finally, 1970's offering was taped in Atlanta, on July 4, with Billy Cox and Mitch Mitchell.

At Stockholm, The Experience were still confined by the conventions of the era – that is, no unseemly jamming, nothing too unfamiliar in the repertoire, and a fair smattering of hit singles in the set. There were moments, notably on 'I Don't Live Today', when their internal cohesion came close to collapse, while the tentative introduction to 'Burning Of The Midnight Lamp' revealed that this was their first live rendition of the song. But 'Midnight Lamp' gradually grew in confidence, and the set ended with a tumultuous 'Purple Haze', as Jimi coaxed barbaric howls from his guitar, and then slid from the barrage of feedback into the loping riff that underpinned the song.

Within a few months, The Experience were in Paris, delivering a set that could hardly have been more different. The pop ambience of the '67 show was gone, and in its place Hendrix asserted his blues roots – opening with a remarkable double whammy of Howlin' Wolf's 'Killing Floor' and Muddy Waters' 'Catfish Blues', the latter clearly spotlighting Jimi's own 'Voodoo Chile' in the distance.

The set also included a fine 'Red House', while the instrumental 'Driving South' mightn't have matched the fury of the 'Radio One' rendition, but still added another layer of potent rock guitar to a compelling concert. Once again, Jimi climaxed with an ocean of sound and 'Purple Haze'.

Fast forward another year, and The Experience were treading water. San Diego in 1969 was a step into the past, as Jimi returned to his back catalogue for 'Fire' and 'Hey Joe'. An intricate 'Spanish Castle Magic' led briefly into 'Sunshine Of Your Love', while a slow, spacey 'Red House' (first heard on 'Hendrix In The West') was the show's finest moment. It was rivalled by 'I Don't Live Today' (premièred on 'The Jimi Hendrix Concerts'), which he used as the foundation for some stunning sonic experimentation. But the closing flurry of 'Purple Haze' and 'Voodoo Child' (interrupted by the exuberance of the crowd) couldn't quite extend that mood.

Where the crowd led in '69, Hendrix, Billy Cox and Mitch Mitchell followed a year later. The Independence Day show in Atlanta proves either (a) that Jimi loved performing that summer and cast all his musical inhibitions to the wind or (b) that he felt so trapped by the constant demands of his international audience that he made little effort to disguise his contempt and boredom. Or possibly (c) both of the above.

'Fire' was the case for the defence, as Hendrix romped through a rendition of the song that swamped the '67 attempt. Ditto 'Spanish Castle Magic', with its long, playful solo. But 'Hear My Train A-Comin' ', despite being stretched to ten minutes in search of inspiration, never matched the beauty of the take on 'Rainbow Bridge'; while 'Stone Free' was a stone mess from start to finish.

The key evidence was 'Star Spangled Banner' – at Woodstock in 1969 a soulful cry of despair at America's political direction, at Atlanta a year later the vehicle for four minutes of guitar hysterics that had all the reverence of a whoopee cushion in a cathedral. From there, 'Straight Ahead' and 'Room Full Of Mirrors' were no more than throwaways, and even 'Voodoo Child (Slight Return)' couldn't survive the show's slaphappy, carefree spirit.

THE CDs: Tape collectors complained that at

least three of the four concerts on 'Stages' weren't taken from the best available sources; that the order of the 1967 and 1970 songs had been altered, for no apparent reason; and that the 1969 and 1970 shows were incomplete. In particular, the disappearance of 'Foxy Lady' from San Diego was baffling, as it would easily have fitted onto the CD.

For the novice, the sound quality of all four shows comes some way short of 'professional' expectations, with the Paris 1968 gig especially muddy. But the sheer historical and musical value of the set far outweighs these considerations.

THE ULTIMATE EXPERIENCE
POLYDOR 517 235-2 (UK), NOVEMBER 1992
Tracks: All Along The Watchtower/Purple Haze/Hey Joe/The Wind Cries Mary/ Angel/ Voodoo Child (Slight Return)/Foxy Lady/The Burning Of The Midnight Lamp/ Highway Chile/Crosstown Traffic/Castles Made Of Sand/Long Hot Summer Night/Red House/ Manic Depression/Gypsy Eyes/Little Wing/ Fire/Wait Until Tomorrow/Star Spangled Banner/Wild Thing

THE ALBUM: When Polydor want a new stu-

dio record from the pre-Beatles instrumental combo The Shadows, they apparently poll members of the public to discover which easy-on-the-ear tunes they'd like the boys to cover next. 'The Ultimate Experience' was apparently compiled via similar methods, so it's surprising not to find Hendrix performing 'My Way' or 'Bohemian Rhapsody' on this CD. And the market research which determined that the (by Jimi's standards) lacklustre 'Wait Until Tomorrow' belonged in this company would have to be seen to be believed.

Otherwise, this is a reasonably sensible selection, made up entirely of studio recordings until the final double-whammy of 'Star Spangled Banner' (Woodstock, of course) and 'Wild Thing' (auto-destruction of guitar at Monterey). 'Red House', for those keeping track of these things, is the version from the US 'Smash Hits' LP, not Jimi's choice from his first album: Douglas repeated the same decision when he prepared the ultimate 'Are You Experienced' for 1993 release.

THE CD: The packaging, with its computer-enhanced Gered Mankowitz photo, presaged the 1993 revamps of the first three studio records. The sound quality of the remastered tracks was excellent, except for 'Long Hot Summer Night', which sounded distressingly thin.

CALLING LONG DISTANCE

UNIVIBES UV-1001 (IRELAND), NOVEMBER 1992

Tracks: The Burning Of The Midnight Lamp/Little Miss Lover/Foxy Lady/Catfish Blues/Oh Man, Is This Me Or What (interview)/Purple Haze/Fire/Getting My Heart Back Together Again/Spanish Castle Magic/ Slow Walkin' Talk/Instrumental Improvisation/Hey Baby (The Land Of The New Rising Sun)/Red House

Longtime Hendrix archivist Caesar Glebbeek is the prime mover behind the excellent Hendrix fanzine *Univibes*, one of two (the other is *Jimpress*) European magazines which have been a boon to collectors in the Nineties.

Teetering on the brink of official recognition from the Estate, *Univibes* has pulled off two coups in recent years – exclusive rights to release, for subscribers only, otherwise unreleased Jimi Hendrix recordings. In both cases, 'Calling Long Distance' and the subsequent 'EXP Over Sweden', the material

they've been allowed access to has been below the rigorous checks on sound quality which Alan Douglas would impose on an official mainstream CD release. But *Univibes* subscribers certainly aren't complaining.

The set – which is immaculately packaged, with copious notes and rare photos – is presented in strict chronological order. It opens with one of the first live performances of 'The Burning Of The Midnight Lamp', from Sweden in September 1967, then returns to Britain a month later for an alternate take of 'Little Miss Lover' – complete with additional wah-wah, wolf-whistles and (it's taken from an acetate) crackles.

'Foxy Lady' and 'Catfish Blues' come from Dutch TV, in November 1967; the latter in particular is a brilliant performance, with a swaggering vocal and an ebullient Mitch Mitchell drum solo. An amusing interview from December 1967 is the only non-musical track, before a Canadian 'Purple Haze' from March 1968, with the customary waves of feedback introducing the song.

'Fire' and 'Getting My Heart Back Together' are taken from The Experience's set at the Miami Pop Festival in May 1968, while 'Spanish Castle Magic' is from the Winterland residency of October that year, and was previously available in edited form on the 'Whammy Bar and Finger Grease' instructional CD.

Perhaps the most intriguing track on the album is 'Slow Walking Talk', a song by Soft Machine member Robert Wyatt, taped during Jimi's October 1968 studio sessions in Hollywood. Jimi performed bass on this jazzy cut, having apparently heard Wyatt run through the song only once.

The two minutes of 'Instrumental Improvisation' from summer 1970 is self-explanatory: it's Billy Cox and Hendrix, investigating the melodic potential of a theme that was never completed. 'Calling Long Distance' comes to an end with two tracks from one of Jimi's last gigs, in Copenhagen the week after the Isle of Wight festival. 'Hey Baby (New Rising Sun)' opens with an elegiac overture; the song is almost incidental to this beautiful performance, which fades out as the band slide into 'All Along The Watchtower'. And where else to end but with 'Red House', adding another ten minutes of majestic blues playing to the Hendrix catalogue.

THE EXPERIENCE COLLECTION
MCA MCAD4-10936 (USA), SEPTEMBER 1993

As part of their 'final' revamping of the original Hendrix studio albums, MCA issued this four-CD box set, which included the remastered and repackaged editions of 'Are You Experienced', 'Axis: Bold As Love' and 'Electric Ladyland', alongside the 'definitive' compilation, 'The Ultimate Experience'. It was a brilliant idea, except for the fact that almost every track on the compilation already featured on one or other of the three studio records.

LIVE FOREVER
GUTS & GRACE 521321-2 (USA), 1993

Tracks featuring Hendrix: Message To Love/Fire/I Don't Live Today

Latin guitar hero Carlos Santana launched his own record label, Guts & Grace, with a record that featured live recordings taken from the final concert tours by legendary artists. This was either a heartfelt tribute or a macabre obsession. In Jimi Hendrix's case, it yielded three previously unreleased tracks from his shows at the Berkeley Community

Theater on May 30, 1970 (the occasion on which he performed his classic rendition of 'Johnny B. Goode', captured on 'Hendrix In The West').

Santana was allowed to take 'Message To Love' and 'Fire' from the first show, and 'I Don't Live Today' from the second. Also included on Live Forever were songs by Marvin Gaye ('Joy' and 'What's Going On'), Bob Marley ('Natural Mystic' and 'Exodus'), Stevie Ray Vaughan ('Riviera Paradise') and John Coltrane ('Ogunde').

EXP OVER SWEDEN
UNIVIBES UV 1002 (IRELAND), JANUARY 1994
Tracks: Can You See Me?/Killing Floor/Foxy Lady/Catfish Blues/Hey Joe/Fire/The Wind Cries Mary/Purple Haze/EXP/Up From The Skies/Little Wing/I Don't Live Today
The second subscribers-only package from the excellent *Univibes* Hendrix fanzine, EXP Over Sweden sampled four Swedish performances from four separate Experience tours. For hardcore collectors, this warts-and-all undertaking was far preferable to the sanitised, mass-marketed exercises of the official Estate; but for the general public, the source

tapes raided for this project were just a little too basic for easy listening.

The album opens with an outdoor recording of 'Can You See Me' from the Tivoli Gardens in Stockholm on May 24, 1967 – a wild, wild performance, undercut only by the defiantly low-fi recording quality. From the same venue, but this time an indoor concert hall, we move forward to September 4, 1967, and a seven-song set that falls prey to every form of distortion imaginable – hiss, buzz, wow, flutter, compression, sheer noise – but still delivers an explosive 'Killing Floor', another delta excursion through 'Catfish Blues', then the usual run of hits climaxing in a feedback-strewn 'Purple Haze'.

Four months later, The Experience were back in Stockholm for a show at the Konserthuset, where they unveiled a rare – possibly even unique – live performance of the opening flurry of the 'Axis: Bold As Love' album, the coupling of 'EXP' and 'Up From The Skies', followed by 'Little Wing'. It's a brave, doomed, but still majestic attempt to capture the studio trickery of the LP in a live show, but it suffers from sound quality poorer than any other tracks listed in this book.

Diehard fans would no doubt rather have the medley in appalling sound than not at all.

Finally, we skip forward exactly a year, but move from Stockholm to Gothenburg, where The Experience treat 'I Don't Live Today' to an eight-minute excursion – complete with lengthy drum intro from Mitch Mitchell, and some neat quotes from 'Third Stone From The Sun' during Hendrix's solo.

With its A5 colour booklet detailing the performances with almost too much technical precision, and a sheaf of rare photos of Hendrix in Sweden, this is an essential purchase for those who value musical content over sound quality.

:BLUES
POLYDOR 521 037-2 (UK), APRIL 1994

Tracks: Getting My Heart Back Together Again/Born Under A Bad Sign/Red House/Catfish Blues/Voodoo Chile/Mannish Boy/Once I Had A Woman/Bleeding Heart/Jam 292/Red House/Getting My Heart Back Together Again

When British author Charles Shaar Murray wrote *Crosstown Traffic* in the late Eighties, one of his avowed intentions was to stress that Jimi Hendrix owed as much, if not more, to the black music tradition than to white rock'n'roll. Unbeknown to Murray, his views were echoed by Hendrix Estate curator Alan Douglas. According to archivist and Knack guitarist Bruce Gary, "Alan Douglas has been trying to put together a proper Hendrix blues album since 1974. He went to the archives back then and listened to a lot of material. But he was working on so many projects that it fell by the wayside."

Twenty years later, ':Blues' (yes, that colon is part of the title) emerged as the first major collection of unheard Hendrix studio cuts since either 'Radio One' (if you count the BBC as a studio) or 'Nine To The Universe'. During those five or fourteen years, countless hours of out-takes had been made available on unofficial bootleg releases, demonstrating that the fans wanted to hear more: with ':Blues', they finally got it.

Not that rarity was the sole rationale behind the release. Douglas set out to expose Jimi's roots in black music, from the acoustic blues of the inter-war period to the uptown R&B that co-existed alongside the early Experience releases in the Sixties. The familiar delta picking of 'Hear My Train A-Comin'', first released on the 'Soundtrack Recordings From The Film Jimi Hendrix' LP in 1973, evidenced Jimi's little-seen command of the acoustic idiom, while 'Red House' (the take also available on the latest 'Are You Experienced CD') satisfied the demand for Fifties-style urban blues. 'Catfish Blues' (as first heard on the Univibes CD, 'Calling Long Distance') showed Jimi moving Chicago blues into the acid-rock era, while 'Hear My Train A-Comin'' (the same cut used on 'Rainbow Bridge') remains the pinnacle of Hendrix's extemporised blues soloing.

The unissued tracks fill in some of the detail, and in one case open up new territory. 'Born Under A Bad Sign' was an Albert King R&B hit from 1967, a magnificent blending of Fifties blues and Sixties Southern soul. With the Band Of Gypsys two years later, Hendrix explored the theme, never quite dominating it – this instrumental rendition rambles somewhat – but striking enough moments of inspiration to make the journey worthwhile in its own right.

'Voodoo Chile Blues' follows 'Catfish Blues', the vintage song from which it drew its inspiration. 'Voodoo' is an earlier take from the session which produced the lengthiest cut on 'Electric Ladyland'; Hendrix drags UFO signals from his guitar while Mitch Mitchell, Steve Winwood and Jack Casady vamp behind him.

In theory, Muddy Waters' macho anthem, 'Mannish Boy', was an ideal selection for a Hendrix blues record. But this rendition, begun in April 1969 and overdubbed the following January, is less a document of Jimi's love for Chicago blues than of his inability to transform it into the funk idiom. It shuffles along without a hint of emotional involvement or even technical grace as compensation.

'Once I Had A Woman' is a long – perhaps over-long – alternative to the track issued on 'Midnight Lightning'. Jimi's guitar work is fluid enough, but the band abandon the blues structure several minutes into their jam, without ever finding a more fruitful direction. Not so with the perennial 'Bleeding Heart', familiar from live tapes, but presented here in a studio rendition from March 1969.

'Jelly 292' came from the same session as 'Jam 292', on the Loose Ends album. "It was Alan's title," explains Bruce Gary, "something to distinguish between the tracks. You got jam and you got jelly." Suitably enough, the song's little more than a 50s-style novelty instrumental, souped up for the psychedelic age.

'Electric Church Red House' is the grand title for a rendition of Jimi's blues anthem previously issued on the instructional CD, 'Variations On A Theme'. Unlike most of his extended takes on the song, this was a studio version, cut in October 1968, which rolls gracefully on the back of Hendrix's guitar, and dissolves in a howl of feedback. From there, Douglas cued up that 'Rainbow Bridge' live classic from Berkeley in 1970, ending an excellent – and extremely well-packaged CD – on a majestic note.

:WOODSTOCK
MCA MCACD 11063 (UK), JULY 1994

Tracks: Introduction/Fire/Izabella/Hear My Train A-Comin'/Red House/Jam Back At The House/Voodoo Child (Slight Return)/ Stepping Stone/Star Spangled Banner/ Purple Haze/Woodstock Improvisation/ Villanova Junction/Farewell

"Jimi's greatest performance": that was how

MCA marketed this CD, cunningly issued to catch the tidal wave of Woodstock 25th anniversary hype, and just one of half-a-dozen cash-in – oops, sorry, tie-in – albums which were thrown at the nostalgia-hungry public in time for Woodstock '94.

For about 15 minutes, maybe even 20, the Hendrix hype was justified. With his experimental Gypsy, Sons & Rainbows Band, Jimi and his muse had waved affectionately from passing trains, but never quite locked onto the same track. There were moments when his fingers would flash fluently over the frets, only for the extended back-up crew to drag him back to mediocrity. As the exhausted crowd of half a million trickled away, there were thirty, maybe fifty thousand people there to witness artistry held in chains.

As a potentially brilliant 'Voodoo Child (Slight Return)' foundered into an appalling solo by second guitarist Larry Lee, and the band stumbled into an abortive 'Stepping Stone', Jimi realised that the battle was lost. "You can leave if you want to," he mumbled. "We're just jamming, that's all."

Then an electric brainwave of genius: Jimi quietened the band, and entered the surreal territory of the 'Star-Spangled Banner'. For the next four minutes, he and his guitar were united in an expression of flamboyant pain – simultaneously exhibiting Hendrix's skills, and exorcising demons that could have been national or personal. Like the studio 'Voodoo Child (Slight Return)' or the Berkeley 'Johnny B. Goode', 'Star-Spangled Banner' was a performance that made irrelevant any attempt to separate the man and his music, as his guitar screeched through pained descents and exploded like fireworks over the exhausted remnants of the Woodstock crowd.

Suddenly triumphant, Jimi could crash through 'Purple Haze' without a moment's thought for finesse – then unwind into a thrilling guitar improvisation that wound in circles, teetered on the brink of incoherence, before easing effortlessly into the rehearsed patterns of the beautiful 'Villanova Junction', an exercise in structured melancholy. The finale of 'Hey Joe' was an anti-climax, but also a relief from the intense passion of what had gone before.

The whole saga unwinds on the unofficial CD 'Purple Haze In Woodstock', plus several even more blatant bootlegs. The official ':Woodstock' (yes, that colon again) captures most of it, though it trims a couple of minutes from 'Stepping Stone', and pretends that the closing 'Hey Joe' never happened.

Certainly its sound quality surpasses any of the bootlegs by far, so your response to ':Woodstock' is likely to be conditioned by your attitude towards archive recordings. Musically, it's erratic, from the opening 'Fire' which nearly goes out, through a pedestrian 'Red House' and the instrumental patterns of 'Jam Back At The House' (alias Mitch Mitchell's 'Beginnings'). Historically, it's inaccurate, mangling the order of the first five songs on the CD, and preferring to sidestep the opportunity to present the entire tangled Woodstock performance. Even the opening applause sounds overdubbed. Maybe this is one case where you need the bootleg, in its low-fi glory, and this official release, to choose according to your mood.

APPENDIX: CD SINGLES

ALL ALONG THE WATCHTOWER
POLYDOR 879 583-2 (UK), 1991 (CD SINGLE)

Tracks: All Along The Watchtower/Star Spangled Banner/Come On (Part 1)

A marginally alternate take of 'Come On (Part 1)' was the prime selling point of this single.

ALL ALONG THE WATCHTOWER
POLYDOR PZCD 100 (UK), OCTOBER 1990

Tracks: All Along The Watchtower/Voodoo Child (Slight Return)/Hey Joe/Crosstown Traffic

Four familiar Experience recordings, coinciding with the release of 'Cornerstones'.

CROSSTOWN TRAFFIC
POLYDOR PZCD 71 (UK), APRIL 1990

Tracks: Crosstown Traffic/Voodoo Child (Slight Return)/All Along The Watchtower/Have You Ever Been (To Electric Ladyland)

To cash in on the selection of 'Crosstown Traffic' as music for a Wrangler jeans commercial, Polydor issued this 'Electric Ladyland' track as an A-side. The Estate even put together a wonderful life-in-the-New-York-streets video to match. Interestingly, the songs here are listed as being taken from "the forthcoming CD, 'Wild Thing: The Best Of Jimi Hendrix'," a project which was immediately cancelled when the Estate got to hear about it.

DAY TRIPPER
RYKODISC RCD 31-008 (USA), 1988

Tracks: Driving South/Getting My Heart Back Together Again/Day Tripper

Rykodisc (or perhaps we should blame Alan Douglas) infuriated collectors by issuing 'Radio One', and then releasing alternate takes of the first two songs listed above on this CD single, which wasn't issued in Britain. These are claimed to be un-broadcast outtakes, but they're actually the tracks which were aired in 1967: it's the 'Radio One' versions which were being premièred.

GLORIA

POLYDOR 887 585-2 (GERMANY), 1988

Tracks: Gloria/Hey Joe/Voodoo Child (Slight Return)/Purple Haze

The familiar jam through Van Morrison's song, plus three Experience studio favourites.

GLORIA

POLYDOR 859 715-2 (AUSTRALIA), 1994

Tracks: Gloria/Stone Free/51st Anniversary/ The Stars That Play With Laughing Sam's Dice

'Gloria' is available on 'The Essential Jimi Hendrix', and 'Stars That Play' on Loose Ends, but both those albums have now been disowned by the Hendrix Estate. That's no doubt why they were chosen for this CD single.

HEY JOE

POLYDOR 879 083-2 (UK), 1993

Tracks: Hey Joe/Stone Free/51st Anniversary/Can You See Me

The fruits of the Experience's first few recording sessions in 1966.

THE PEEL SESSIONS

STRANGE FRUIT SFPSCD 065 (UK), DECEMBER 1988

Tracks: Radio One/Day Tripper/Wait Until Tomorrow/Hear My Train A- Comin'/Spanish Castle Magic

Predating the 'Radio One' album by several months, this CD EP featured the entire contents of The Experience's last BBC Radio session, on December 15, 1967. These tracks were broadcast on Top Gear, as presented by John Peel and Tommy Vance – hence the title, and this set's inclusion in a long series of Strange Fruit releases. Shame about the tedious generic artwork, though.

PURPLE HAZE

POLYDOR PZCD 33 (UK), JANUARY 1989

Tracks: Purple Haze/51st Anniversary/All Along The Watchtower/Hey Joe.

Three Experience A-sides, plus the slightly more obscure '51st Anniversary'.

THE WIND CRIES MARY

POLYDOR 863 917-2 (UK), NOVEMBER 1992

Tracks: The Wind Cries Mary/Fire/Foxy Lady/May This Be Love

Four studio tracks, issued alongside The Ultimate Experience.

SECTION 3
UNOFFICIAL CDS

In one sense, 90% or more of the CDs reviewed thus far have been 'unofficial', in the sense that Jimi Hendrix never sanctioned their release. But this section is reserved for albums that have not been okayed by Jimi, his executors, his estate or Alan Douglas, but which have – by some legal loophole or another – managed to flood the marketplace over the last eight years or so.

Almost without exception, the records listed below are musically worthless. Historically, they could boast some minor pretension to significance if (a) they were properly annotated, (b) they were compiled with some sense of their place in Jimi's career, (c) they were cheap and (d) they weren't so bloody repetitious.

Occasionally, they are beautifully packaged, making their low-fi, third-rate contents all the more disappointing. More often, they are as shoddy to view as they are to hear. Unless stated otherwise, my recommendation is to steer well clear of all the CDs detailed in this section.

Releases qualify for this 'unofficial' tag for one or more of the following reasons:

(1) They contain recordings which would never have been okayed for release, or reissue, by Jimi Hendrix. Of course, this also applies to most of the legal, 'official' CDs issued since his death.

(2) They feature tracks whose ownership has become impossible to ascertain, and which have effectively (if not legally) fallen into the public domain (i.e. anyone can release them without the risk of being sued for breach of copyright).

(3) They are made up of official releases by Jimi, which have passed out of copyright in the country where they are being reissued. This applies in particular to Japanese CDs made up of pre-1969 Hendrix studio recordings.

(4) They contain officially unreleased live recordings, which were briefly legal in one or more countries of the world thanks to the complete breakdown of international copyright co-operation in the late Eighties and early Nineties. In almost all cases, it would have been ruled illegal to sell these releases (mostly from Germany and Italy) in the UK, had anyone been bothered to bring a lengthy, protracted and expensive lawsuit to prove the point.

In the world of bootlegs, the mere fact that a record is 'unofficial' (and therefore often illegal) can make the heart of the diehard fan beat a little faster. Sadly, the Hendrix catalogue proves that unofficial and exciting aren't synonyms. There are plenty of unreleased Hendrix gems available on 100% bootleg releases, but those can't and won't be offered for sale in respectable record stores. For the most part, the 'unofficial' recordings included on the 'unofficial' CDs are the dregs of Jimi's career, thrown onto the marketplace with only one aim in mind: to part a fool from his money.

Four groups of 'unofficial' recordings crop up time and time again on the following albums.

(1) THE LONNIE YOUNGBLOOD SESSIONS

Without ever achieving a hit record in his own right, saxophonist and singer Lonnie Youngblood has sold more albums than many more famous performers. Not that he could, or probably would, take much pride in this fact. Aside from his diehard fans in the mid-60s, scarcely a handful of the tens of thousands of people who've purchased Youngblood's 1963 recordings with Jimi Hendrix could have had the slightest interest in Lonnie or his music.

For both men, it was just another session. Youngblood was hustling for a hit single, at a time when the R&B and pop markets were susceptible to anyone who could hit a two-minute groove and make it stick on the dance floor. Towards the end of 1963, Jimi Hendrix was travelling through Philadelphia en route to his dream of fame and riches in New York, when he caught word that Youngblood needed a guitar-player for a recording session.

Jimi doubtless made the most of his touring pedigree, when he'd played back-up behind stars like Jackie Wilson, Little Richard and Sam Cooke in the Southern states.

Youngblood taped around nine or ten tunes with a small R&B band, allowing Hendrix to cut loose with an occasional solo, but mostly restricting him to rhythm work. 'Go Go Place' and 'Go Go Shoes', a blatant dance craze cash-in, appeared as a single on a small local label in December 1963; a month or two later, a second Youngblood 45 appeared, coupling 'Soul Food' with 'Goodbye Bessie Mae'.

None of the other Youngblood material surfaced during Jimi's lifetime. But within months of his death, Maple Records in New York compiled an album called 'Two Great Experiences Together', suggesting that the sessions had actually taken place in 1966. Some of the Hendrix tracks were overdubbed with soundalike lead guitar, while some were edited in several different ways so they could be presented as alternative recordings. Worst of all, Maple made up the numbers with tracks which had no Hendrix involvement.

In the CD age, Maple's album looks like a work of genius. None of the CDs which include the Youngblood recordings (a) feature all of the tracks Jimi and Lonnie taped together, or (b) resist the temptation of including non-Hendrix recordings as well. All the Youngblood

CDs are credited entirely to Jimi, and all of them feature 'fake' Hendrix recordings. No-one has been more appalled by this trickery than Youngblood himself, but he has no legal power to prevent the charade continuing.

(2) THE CURTIS KNIGHT RECORDINGS

In the years after Jimi's death, by far the most prolific source of 'unofficial' Hendrix releases were his two stints of recording with another would-be R&B star of the mid-Sixties, Curtis Knight. Using the pseudonym Jimmy James, Hendrix was a member of his band from just October to December 1965, but during that time he helped Knight record around a dozen studio tracks, and was also taped on stage at two, possibly more, New York club shows.

In October 1965, in fact, Jimi signed an exclusive recording deal with Knight's recording boss, Ed Chalpin of PPX Records. This came back to haunt him after he found fame in England, when PPX pressed Track/Polydor for legal recompense for Hendrix's alleged breach of contract.

Jimi did nothing to calm the legal waters by naïvely agreeing to return to PPX in July/August 1967 and take part in another

Curtis Knight session, during which a further 12 tracks were taped.

Knight issued two singles from the PPX recordings around the start of 1966; then, after the success of 'Hey Joe' and 'Purple Haze', several singles and albums of Knight/Hendrix recordings were prepared for release. When Jimi died, the live tapes of the duo in action were also thrown onto the market in equally haphazard fashion.

In theory, there should be scores of 'unofficial' Knight/Hendrix CDs on the market, but in fact, only a tiny fraction of the potential material has appeared on compact disc – and then only the studio recordings, which do at least have some historical and musical interest on their side. It's a gap in the exploitation market that surely won't survive for long.

(3) THE SCENE CLUB JAM

Early March 1968, and Jimi's on stage, as usual. Tonight the venue is the Scene Club on West 46th Street, in the heart of Manhattan, where proprietor and (appropriately enough) scene-maker Steve Paul has gathered a cast of luminaries for an early-hours jam session. Alongside Jimi are members of The McCoys, the Scene's house band — yep, the same McCoys who graced us with 'Hang On Sloopy' three years earlier.

Though Jimi's just jamming, that's all, he's running a tape machine off the primitive mixing desk. If he'd known that the scarcely coherent results of the evening's exclusive entertainment would be released again and again and again, twenty years after his death, he'd have pushed the 'off' switch fast. Instead, posterity has been gifted with a version of 'Red House' that epitomises grace under pressure, plus a less impressive 'Bleeding Heart', and plenty of lazy guitar interplay.

So far, so good, but among the Scene in-crowd is James Douglas Morrison, lead singer with The Doors, and on this night auditioning for a role as the biggest asshole in the universe. He's a star, so he has to crawl on stage and attract someone's attention. He bellows down the microphone, delivering a flurry of slurred expletives, and then collapses in a whisky-sodden heap, taking Jimi's mike-stand with him. Hendrix plays on, as if it's just another day on the edge of the apocalypse.

Fun to hear once, purgatory beyond that:

so why has this non-event reappeared more times than the knife-maniac in 'Halloween'?

(4) THE EXPERIENCE AT THE ALBERT HALL

February 24, 1969: the venue is the Royal Albert Hall, and the event is only The Jimi Hendrix Experience's second live show in England since the Woburn Abbey festival the previous June (the first 'comeback' gig had been in the same prestigious concert hall, six days earlier). Priced out of the UK market by manager Mike Jeffery's demands from promoters, Hendrix had agreed to the shows because he realised that The Experience were in danger of puncturing the core of their British support by their relative lack of activity.

Film director Joe Levine captures the show, during which The Experience are augmented by Traffic members Steve Winwood and Chris Wood, for a movie provisionally entitled The Last Experience. And so it proved to be – in Britain, at least, though the original Hendrix/Redding/Mitchell trio survived a few months longer in the States.

The movie remains unreleased to this day, wrapped up in legal hassles, but that didn't prevent Ember Records issuing two 'soundtrack' albums in the early Sixties, 'Experience' and 'More Experience'. Both LPs were taken direct from the film audio track, not professionally recorded tapes, and their sound quality suffered accordingly. Since then, the same material has been issued on a dozen or more unofficial CDs, while the Hendrix estate has dipped into material from the same source (notably on the 'Red House: Reflections On A Theme' album).

Ember set another unfortunate precedent back in 1971, when they claimed that 'Experience' contained "probably the last recorded sounds of Jimi Hendrix". The same laughably incorrect statement has appeared on several 'unofficial' CDs, as has the erroneous claim that the Albert Hall show was the Last Experience Concert.

ABTONE SESSIONS
JIMCO JICK 89273 (JAPAN), 1993
Tracks: Good Times/Voices/Suspicious/ Whipper/Bessie Mae/Soul Food/Voice In The Wind/Free Spirit/Hot Trigger/Psycho/ Come On Baby Parts 1 & 2/Night Life/You Got It

Astonishingly expensive (the usual import price is around £25), 'Abtone Sessions' is Hendrix exploitation at its worst. Of the 14 tracks, all featuring saxophonist Lonnie Youngblood, Jimi performs on (at most) five – the dual helping of 'Come On Baby', plus 'Whipper' (actually 'Wipe This Sweat'), "Bessie Mae' and 'Soul Food'. There's a flicker or two of guitar genius, plus around 40 minutes of forgettable 1963 R&B, much of it overdubbed in the Seventies by a hamfisted imitator to suggest that Jimi was around for the whole shebang.

BAND OF GYPSYS
ON STAGE CD 12022 (ITALY), 1993
Tracks: Power Of Soul/We Gotta Live Together/Changes/Message To Love/ Machine Gun/Who Knows

A brilliant idea: the tracks from the official 'Band Of Gypsys' CD, presented in a different order, with cheapskate packaging. In Britain, it would have been persecuted as a bootleg, but the complications of European Community law in the early Nineties allowed this set to appear at budget price across the Continent, and then be surreptitiously imported back into Britain as a legitimate release. Needless to say, it's not, and the sound quality proves it.

THE BEST AND REST OF JIMI HENDRIX
ACTION REPLAY CDAR 1022 (UK), MARCH 1991
Tracks: Red House/Bleeding Heart/ Tomorrow Never Knows/Woke Up This Morning And Found Yourself Dead/ Morrison's Lament/Uranus Rock/The Sunshine Of Your Love

The Scene Club jam in all its dubious glory, and not even the complete recording, at that. Definitely more 'rest' than 'best', even at budget price.

BEST OF ARTIST SELECTION
JASREC JECD 1030 (JAPAN), 1993
Tracks: Purple Haze/Fire/The Wind Cries Mary/Can You See Me/51st Anniversary/

Hey Joe/Stone Free/The Stars That Play With Laughing Sam's Dice/Manic Depression/ Highway Chile/Burning Of The Midnight Lamp/Foxy Lady/Remember/Third Stone From The Sun

Stunning title, equally impressive artwork, which doesn't bother to illustrate Jimi or anything relating to him. These are the original Experience studio recordings, presented in less than perfect quality, as an exercise in unnecessary repackaging.

BIG ARTIST SELECTION
PIGEON GX-448 (JAPAN), 1993

Tracks: Purple Haze/Third Stone From The Sun/51st Anniversary/Burning Of The Midnight Lamp/Can You See Me/Fire/ Foxy Lady/Hey Joe/Highway Chile/Manic Depression/Remember/ Stars That Play With Laughing Sam's Dice/Stone Free/The Wind Cries Mary

How do they dream up these titles? And why does the cover show a car, a street-sign and a clock? Maybe Jimi was meant to turn up for a photo session, but overslept. You would too, if you had to plough through another entirely random selection of Experience studio tracks.

BLEEDING HEART (1 DISC OF 4-CD SET BLACK AND WHITE BLUES)
CASTLE MBSCD 431 (UK), 1994

Tracks: Red House/Bleeding Heart/ Tomorrow Never Knows/Woke Up This Morning And Found Yourself Dead/ Morrison's Lament/Uranus Rock/The Sunshine Of Your Love

Look, if you really have to own the Scene Club jam, then this is where you should buy it. 'Black And White Blues' is a low-budget box set which teams Jimi's most over-exposed half-hour with CDs by Fleetwood Mac (live in 1968, when their blueswailing tendencies were at their zenith), John Lee Hooker and Alexis Korner. The packaging is minimal, but the set works out at £2.50 per CD, which even for the Scene Club is something of a bargain.

CAFE AU GO GO JAM SESSION
KOINE K880802 (ITALY), FEBRUARY 1989

Tracks: Beginning Of A Jam/Monday Jam/Jimi Jam/Swing Jimi Jam/Funky Jam/ Jamming Wing

Only the most lenient of copyright laws – as

found in late Eighties Italy – would allow the 'legal' release of this album, documenting a lacklustre jam session at New York's Cafe Au Go Go in March 1968, within a week or two of the infamous Scene Club jam.

On stage alongside Jimi were musicians like Buddy Miles, Harvey Brooks, Paul Butterfield and Elvin Bishop, but even such a selection of late Sixties rock/blues luminaries couldn't be relied upon to produce an evening of sparkling improvisation. Like the Scene Club tape, this is amusing to hear once, but that's all.

The brilliantly inventive song titles on this (very) semi-official CD disguise the fact that among the songs performed that night in New York were 'Everything's Gonna Be Alright' (as at the Scene), 'Stormy Monday', 'Little Wing' and an early version of what became '3 Little Bears'.

Finally, check the cover of this CD: is that supposed to be Jimi Hendrix or Little Richard?

CHEROKEE
DOG 'N' ROLL DNR 001 (ITALY), 1994
Tracks: Good Times/Voices/Suspicious/

Whipper/Goodbye, Bessie Mae/Soul Food/Voice In The Wind/Free Spirit
Jimi's father's mother was the daughter of an Irishman and a Cherokee Indian – hence the title of this set, attractively packaged in a circular tin featuring an appropriate Hendrix caricature. Unfortunately, there's a CD inside, which includes a not exactly generous eight tracks by Lonnie Youngblood. Three of them ('Whipper', 'Soul Food' and 'Goodbye, Bessie Mae') feature the 21-year-old Hendrix on erratic guitar. Five don't. Now you tell me why anyone should buy this – except maybe for the sheer joy of owning a record on the Dog 'N' Roll label.

COLLECTION
GRAFFITI GRCD 13 (SWITZERLAND), AUGUST 1990
Tracks: Spanish Castle Magic/Star Spangled Banner/Purple Haze/Foxy Lady/I Don't Live Today/Voodoo Child (Slight Return)/The Sunshine Of Your Love/Red House
Once again, the vagaries of European law allowed UK stores to import this disc, whereas if it had been released in Britain, they'd have been marched off to court to face the wrath of the British Phonographic Institute.

This set wasn't so much a 'Collection' as a document of Jimi's show at the LA Forum in April 1969. The entire set, minus 'Foxy Lady', appeared as a 'bonus' CD with the official US box, 'Lifelines'. 'Foxy Lady' appears here, but 'Tax Free' doesn't. Therefore, you have to buy 'Lifelines' and 'Collection' to obtain the whole show. Or you can buy one of the bootlegs which include the entire thing. And they wonder why people prefer bootlegs...

COLLECTION
THE COLLECTION COL 017 (HOLLAND), 1993

Tracks: Little Wing/Purple Haze/Voodoo Child (Slight Return)/Red House/Wild Thing/The Sunshine Of Your Love/Bleeding Heart/Soul Food/Fire/Room Full Of Mirrors/Psycho/Let Me Go/Freedom And You/Good Feeling/Go Go Shoes/She's So Fine/Sweet Thang/Win Your Love/Two Into One Goes/Voice In The Wind

'+75 Min.', it boasts on the cover of this ramshackle 'semi-official' CD. In other words, never mind the quality, or the contents, feel the length. Well, size isn't everything, especially when the idiot compiler of this album chooses to combine tracks from The Jimi Hendrix Experience's eventful Royal Albert Hall show from February 24, 1969, with Lonnie Youngblood performances, most of which have no connection with our man. Worse still, he or she even manages to slip one of the 1963 recordings, 'Soul Food', into the midst of the live set. A brilliant subversion of listeners' expectations, no doubt.

For the record, the following cuts carry no Hendrix guitar or vocals: 'Psycho', 'Freedom And You', 'Good Feeling', 'She's So Fine', 'Win Your Love', 'Two Into One Goes' and 'Voice In The Wind'. Meanwhile, the Albert Hall show is best (if incompletely) heard on one of the semi-official CDs bearing a title like 'Experience'. One day, the legal hassles will be solved and the entire gig will appear on an official CD. Then again, CDs may well have been phased out by then.

THE COLLECTION
OBJECT OR 0071 (UK), 1990

Tracks: Flashing/Hornet's Nest/Don't Accuse Me/Simon Says/Day Tripper/ Welcome Home/Strange Things/Odd Ball/All I Want/Whoaech/Down Mean Blues/Monday Morning Blues/Bring My

Baby Back/Suspicious/Good Times/Hot Trigger/Psycho/Good Feeling

Original title, yes? And an original concept: let's rip off the punters. The case for the defence, first of all: this was a budget CD. And the prosecution? This is a total ragbag of Hendrix trivia, featuring eight tracks with Curtis Knight; one ('All I Want', better known as 'Soul Food') with Lonnie Youngblood; one more ('Whoaech', alias 'Tomorrow Never Knows') from the cacophonous Scene Club jam of March 1968; and six which have no trace of Jimi whatsoever.

For once, though, there's a bonus, albeit a dubious one. Appearing here for just about the only time on a (semi-)legal CD are two tracks taken from a 1972 album titled hopefully 'Jimi Hendrix At His Best Volume 2'. Along with its companions (Volumes 1 & 3, surprisingly enough), these supposedly featured Jimi's first ever recordings. In fact, they documented a home jam session from September 1969, four weeks after Woodstock, between Jimi, percussionist Juma Sultan and saxophonist Mike Ephron.

After being roundly savaged in reviews of the time, these three albums vanished, and

so did their contents – meandering instrumentals, for the most part, with spurious titles. Eighteen years later, here were 'Down Home Blues' and 'Monday Morning Blues' making a reappearance, and begging a question: when there are so many crap Hendrix CDs on the market, how come no-one has ever reissued the material from all three of the 'At The Best' LPs? (Don't even think about the other question, which is why anyone would want to hear them.)

THE CRAZY WORLD OF JIMI HENDRIX
JIMCO JICK 89329 (JAPAN), 1994

Tracks: The Sunshine Of Your Love/Voodoo Chile (Slight Return)/Purple Haze/Little Wing/Tomorrow Never Knows/Bleeding Heart/Morrison's Lament/The Sunshine Of Your Love/Soul Food/Goodbye, Bessie Mae/Come On Baby Part 1/Come On Baby Part 2

Oh, the crazy world of Jimi Hendrix – doesn't it make you want to throw your hands in the air with the joy of it all? Not when you have to pay an emperor's ransom for this load of garbage, it doesn't.

From the top then: the first four tracks

come from the Albert Hall gig, February 1969; the next four from the Scene Club, March 1968; then there's four by Jimi and Lonnie Youngblood from 1963. The cover lettering swirls in an attractively psychedelic way, but 'The Crazy World' retails in Britain at more than £35. Exploitative crap.

CROSSTOWN CONVERSATION
TABAK CBAK 4082 (UK), JUNE 1994

Track: Jimi Hendrix Interview 1970
Early 1970: Hendrix's manager, Mike Jeffery, realises that his man's profile is in danger of being submerged by the long delay in fresh studio product since 'Electric Ladyland'. On New Year's Day, while Jimi was preparing for his Band Of Gypsys shows at the Fillmore East, Jeffery rang Noel Redding in London, and invited him to rejoin The Experience.

Hendrix's role in this plot is difficult to establish, but on February 4, Jimi, Noel and Mitch Mitchell were duly presented to Rolling Stone reporter John Burks, for an exclusive interview in which he could reveal the reunion of the original Hendrix trio to the world.

As Burks discovered, Jimi was as bewildered as anyone by the plans to relaunch The Experience, and could offer no concrete timetable for concerts or recording sessions. Instead, he spoke softly but earnestly about the failures of The Band Of Gypsys, and the problems of transporting his musical ideas from his mind to his guitar.

'Crosstown Conversation' is one of several CDs featuring extracts from this interview: this selection runs for just under 30 minutes, and is identical to the same company's 'Introspective'. Check 'Jimi Hendrix 1970' for a longer cut of Burks' encounter.

EARLY CLASSICS
PAIR SCD 4926 (USA)

Tracks: Get That Feeling/How Would You Feel/Hush Now/No Business/Simon Says/ Gotta Have A New Dress/Strange Things/ Welcome Home/Love Love/Day Tripper/ Gloomy Monday/Fool For You Baby/Happy Birthday/Don't Accuse Me/Hornet's Nest/ Flashing/Odd Ball
In the years after Jimi's death, record stores were crammed with budget albums repeating the same sorry selection of Curtis Knight songs, all featuring guitar by Hendrix. In the CD age, it's the Lonnie Youngblood

material that's dominated the release sheets, making this set of Knight tracks not altogether unwelcome.

Many of the songs were taped at Studio 76 in New York during Jimi's stint as a member of Knight's band, late in 1965: these cuts include 'How Would You Feel', a blatant rewrite of Bob Dylan's 'Like A Rolling Stone', and still probably the most exciting Hendrix/Knight collaboration of them all. There are also several tracks recorded in July/August 1967, when Jimi was conned/persuaded/encouraged (depending on whom you believe) back into Studio 76, either to fulfil his contract with PPX Records, or to jam with his old buddies.

'Classics' is probably taking things too far, but almost every track does have a flicker of the man's genius, albeit surrounded by second-rate soul singing from Knight. Worth buying if it's cheap.

THE EARLY JIMI HENDRIX – LIVE
FORTUNE 3179 (GERMANY), 1993
Tracks: Good Times/Voice/Suspicious/ Whipper/Goodbye Bessie Mae/Soul Food/ Voice In The Wind/Free Spirit

Live? Only in the sense that Jimi Hendrix wasn't dead when these Lonnie Youngblood tracks were recorded. Sadly, he wasn't in the studio, either, for five out of the eight – see 'Cherokee' for full details. Fortune's set has one 'bonus', though: overdubbed applause. Anyone who recognises their handclaps should sue for libel, as they would only have applauded this garbage under torture.

EXPERIENCE
BULLDOG BDCD 40023 (UK), JANUARY 1987
Tracks: Little Wing/Voodoo Child (Slight Return)/Room Full Of Mirrors/Fire/Purple Haze/Bleeding Heart/The Sunshine Of Your Love/Room Full Of Mirrors/Bleeding Heart/Smashing Of Amps

In theory, this two-LPs-on-one-CD coupling of the 'Experience' and 'More Experience' albums from the early Seventies should be a blessing. Hendrix appears on every track, for starters, and both albums capture an erratic but often explosive performance by the original Experience line-up – performing live at the Royal Albert Hall in February 1969.

There's one drawback, though. When Ember issued the original LPs in 1971 and

1972, they were so short of raw material that they included edited versions of two songs from the first album on the second as well. And Bulldog, paying no attention to their product, repeated the sin on this CD. Only two tracks separate 'Bleeding Heart' (incompetent edit) from 'Bleeding Heart' (complete). Worse still, the inferior sound quality of the original tapes is retained in all its dubious glory here.

Intrigued by that 'Smashing Of Amps'? It's a one-off performance, certainly, but not one Jimi would ever have wanted to repeat. Not so much a song, in fact, more a total failure and then destruction of equipment. Makes good white noise, though.

EXPERIENCE
SIGNAL CD 88110 (HOLLAND)
Tracks: *Red House/Voodoo Child (Slight Return)/She's So Fine/Bleeding Heart/ Fire/Purple Haze/Room Full Of Mirrors/ Suspicious/Smashing Of Amps/Wild Thing/ Something You Got/The Sunshine Of Your Love*
Oh dear. Poorly mastered tracks from the Albert Hall show, added to a couple of Lonnie

Youngblood cuts on which Jimi doesn't appear, and a version of the Chris Kenner R&B hit – presumably by Curtis Knight – which is also a bit lacking in the Hendrix department. One experience to avoid, in fact.

EXPERIENCE
JIMCO JICK 89371 (JAPAN), 1994
Tracks: *The Sunshine Of Your Love/Room Full Of Mirrors/Bleeding Heart/Smashing Of Amps*
A straight reissue of the original 1971 album from the Royal Albert Hall, complete with Ember's artwork. Ridiculously expensive, and totally pointless.

EXPERIENCE AT ROYAL ALBERT HALL
JIMCO JICK 89100 (JAPAN), 1993
Tracks: *The Sunshine Of Your Love/Room Full Of Mirrors/Little Wing/Voodoo Child (Slight Return)/Purple Haze/Fire/Wild Thing/Bleeding Heart/Smashing Of Amps*
That 1969 concert again, this time without the duplication of the Bulldog Experience CD. Still a low-fi listening experience, though, with the most witless cover (non-)artwork on any of these unofficial releases.

EXPERIENCES
PULSAR PULS 004 (EUROPE), 1991

Tracks: Voices/Let Me Go/Gangster Of Love/Win Your Love/Two + One Goes/ Freedom And You/Good Times/Voice In The Wind/She's So Fine/Soul Food

Lonnie Youngblood again, occasionally with a tentative Jimi Hendrix on guitar – a total waste of time, in other words. It's difficult to imagine many experiences worse than this one.

FIRE
THE ENTERTAINERS CD 297 (ITALY), 1993

Tracks: Fire/Manic Depression/Sunshine Of Your Love/Killing Floor/Tax Free/Foxy Lady/Little Wing/Lover Man/Hey Joe/Purple Haze/Wild Thing

"Live Performances" is what the cover of this cheapo-cheapo effort promises, and what it delivers as well – all pinched from the official 'Live At Winterland' release, except for 'Little Wing' (Albert Hall) and 'Lover Man' (Berkeley), which come from 'Hendrix In The West'. Sound quality here is vastly inferior to the legitimate releases.

THE FIRST RECORDINGS
OVERSEAS TECX 20651 (JAPAN), 1994

Tracks: Good Feeling/Go Go Shoes/Bring My Baby Back/Psycho/Come On Baby/Blues Blues/Sweet Thang/Lime Lime/Peoples Peoples/Whoaech/ Night Life/Nobody Can Change Me/You Got It

At least the title is correct – up to a point. Three of these tracks, 'Go Go Shoes', 'Come On Baby' and 'Sweet Thang', are indeed from Hendrix's first recording sessions, with our old chum Lonnie Youngblood. Four more tracks, 'Blues Blues', 'Lime Lime', 'Peoples Peoples' and 'Whoaech', are taken from that perennial peril, the Scene Club jam of March 1968 – and all given spurious titles. That leaves six Lonnie Youngblood songs that may have been his first recordings, but certainly weren't Jimi's.

FREE SPIRIT
THUNDERBOLT CDTB 094 (UK), JANUARY 1991

Tracks: Good Times/Voices/Suspicious/ Whipper/Goodbye Bessie Mae/Soul Food/Voice In The Wind/Free Spirit

The eight songs from 'Cherokee' and 'The Early Jimi Hendrix – Live', in yet another permutation. This one sold at full-price, with artwork that made low-budget seem like a compliment. Thunderbolt, whose catalogue includes equally deceptive releases by Sly Stone, Alice Cooper and Aretha Franklin, also issued a companion CD, 'Nightlife'. Avoid both at all costs.

GANGSTER OF LOVE
ARC TOP 124 (UK), 1993

Tracks: Gangster Of Love/Let Me Go/Voice In The Wind/Two And One Goes/Good Times/From This Day On/Soul Food/Freedom And You/Win Your Love/Voices

Budget price, at least, this time – but still only two Jimi Hendrix appearances in the 30-minute running time (on 'Let Me Go' and 'Soul Food'). For Lonnie Youngblood completists and naïve idiots only.

GOLD
GOLD 022 (HOLLAND), 1994

Tracks: Purple Haze/Voodoo Child (Slight Return)/Little Wing/Wild Thing/Red House/The Sunshine Of Your Love/ Voices/ Gangster Of Love/She's So Fine/Soul Food/Win Your Love/Voice In The Wind/ Psycho/Good Times

Fool's gold, in fact, as this recycles the diet of Albert Hall tracks (five), the Scene Club jam ('Red House') and Lonnie Youngblood epics (only 'Soul Food' featuring Hendrix).

GOLD COLLECTION
DIGITAL DEJA 2 D2CD03 (ITALY), 1992

Tracks: Foxy Lady/I Don't Live Today/Red House/Spanish Castle Magic/Star Spangled Banner/The Wind Cries Mary/The Burning Of The Midnight Lamp/Fire/Purple Haze/ Voodoo Child (Slight Return)/The Sunshine Of Your Love/Catfish Blues/Killing Floor/Can You Please Crawl Out Your Window/Hey Joe

Wot no Lonnie Youngblood? It's true – in fact, there's nothing on this double-CD of dubious legality in the UK from the Albert Hall or the Scene Club, either.

At its usual retail price of around £7, it's actually something of a bargain, despite its total lack of annotation or explanation of its contents. In strictly chronological order, they are as follows: 'The Wind Cries Mary', 'Burning Of The Midnight Lamp' and 'Fire' come from the Stockholm concert in September 1967 which is available in far more acceptable quality on the official 'Stages' box set. The following month, the Jimi Hendrix Experience taped their arrangement of Bob Dylan's 'Can You Please Crawl Out Your Window' for Alexis Korner's Rhythm & Blues BBC radio show. Omitted from the 'Radio One' collection of Beeb sessions, it's a welcome inclusion here.

Moving forward another month to November 1967, we're in Holland, for 'Experiencing The Blues' – a bootlegger's title for the song we've come to know and love as 'Catfish Blues'. 'Calling Long Distance' and ':Blues' now feature this track with improved sound reproduction.

Next we move North to Stockholm, and on in time to January 1969: from two shows at the city's Concert Hall come ripping versions of Howlin' Wolf's 'Killin' Floor' and 'Hey Joe' – otherwise unavailable on anything approaching an 'official' release. The remainder of this set features The Experience's entire set from the LA Forum in April 1969, minus 'Tax Free' – the same material that appears on the Swiss CD 'Collection', in fact.

GOLDEN BEST
LILY NLC-64 (JAPAN), 1993

Tracks: Purple Haze/Foxy Lady/Hey Joe/Fire/Can You See Me/Highway Chile/Burning Of The Midnight Lamp/Third Stone From The Sun/51st Anniversary/Remember/ The Wind Cries Mary/Manic Depression

The Japanese record business at its most environmentally conscious, recycling The Experience's first few months in the studio without wasting a morsel of brain power or imagination. Great cover: it shows a branch of the Hard Rock Café. I only hope the restaurant charged them for the privilege.

GOOD FEELING
OBJECT OR 0149 (UK)

Tracks: Good Feeling/Go Go Shoes/Bring My Baby Back/Psycho/Come On Baby/Baby Baby/Sweet Thang/Lime Lime/Peoples Peoples/Whoa'ech/Night Life/Nobody Can Change Me/You Got It

This is the British equivalent of the appalling Japanese CD, 'The First Recordings'. A good feeling for accountants only.

GOOD TIMES
MUSIC REFLEXION 1421.2004-2 (GERMANY), 1994

Tracks: Good Times/Voices/Suspicious/ Whipper/Bessie Mae/Soul Food/Voice In The Wind/Free Spirit/Good Feeling/Hot Trigger/Psycho/Come On Baby Pt. 1/Come On Baby Pt. 2/Night Life/You Got It/Wake Up In The Morning/Lime Lime/Peoples Peoples/Whoa'ech

By now you can recognise this stuff for yourself, surely – Youngblood plus the Scene Club, adding up to another CD that never comes close to matching its title.

GREAT HITS U.S.A.
JASREC GH-1841 (JAPAN), 1993

Tracks: Purple Haze/Fire/The Wind Cries Mary/Can You See Me/51st Anniversary/ Hey Joe/Stone Free/The Stars That Play With Laughing Sam's Dice/Manic Depression/Highway Chile/Burning Of The Midnight Lamp/Foxy Lady

Yes, you can buy these tracks on scores of other Japanese CDs, but look on the bright side – at least they do feature Jimi Hendrix. The early Experience studio sides, one more time – recorded in England, despite the title.

HENDRIX
ROYAL COLLECTION RC 83113 (HOLLAND), 1993

Tracks: Good Feeling/Go Go Shoes/Bring My Baby Back/Psycho/Come On Baby I/Come On Baby II/Blue Blues/Sweet Thang/Lime Lime/Peoples Peoples/Whoa Ech/Night Life/Nobody Can Change Me/You Got It

The dreadfully tacky cover should be warning enough: for the contents, see under 'The First Recordings, Good Feeling' or complete rip-off.

HENDRIX SPEAKS
RHINO R2 70771 (USA), OCTOBER 1990

Tracks: Interviews with Jimi Hendrix by Meatball Fulton (1967) and Nancy Carter (1969)

Just over 45 minutes of authentic Hendrix interviews, taped in London in December 1967, and in California in June 1969. The Fulton encounter is fascinatingly free-form – Hendrix recalls a childhood dream about his mother vanishing on a camel, mentions his interest in the supernatural, and voices his misgivings about the process whereby his music reached the street: "It makes me so mad. We record it and everything, and then all of a sudden something happens and it just comes out all screwed up."

The Carter interview is less thrilling, though Hendrix rises above some uninspired questioning to express himself on the subject of the American education system. But other conversations from the same period (like the piece written by Jerry Hopkins in *Rolling Stone*) are probably more informative.

HEY JOE
LEGEND WZ 90025 (GERMANY), 1994

Tracks: Hey Joe/Foxy Lady/Still Raining, Still Dreaming/Little Miss Strange/Third Stone From The Sun/Can You See Me/Night Bird Flying/Love Or Confusion/Have You Ever Been (To Electric Ladyland)/Red House/Are You Experienced/May This Be Love/ Angel/ Voodoo Child (Slight Return)/Purple Haze/ Gypsy Eyes

The cover photo showing Hendrix as a right-handed guitarist doesn't inspire confidence, but the contents are an interesting, if hardly definitive, collection of 1966-1970 studio recordings, in not quite perfect quality. It's at least a change from the array of Japanese compilations concentrating on 1966-67 material, however.

HISTORIC HENDRIX
PAIR SPCD2 1155 (JAPAN), 1986

Tracks: Get That Feeling/How Would You Feel/Hush Now/No Business/Simon Says/Gotta Have A New Dress/Strange Things/Welcome Home/Love Love/Day Tripper/Gloomy Monday/Fool For You Baby/Happy Birthday/Don't Accuse Me/ Hornet's Nest/Flashing/Odd Ball

The Japanese equivalent of the US CD 'Early Classics', with a very slightly more appropriate title for this ragbag of Curtis Knight recordings.

THE INTERVIEW
CID PRODUCTIONS CID 006 (UK)

Track: Jimi Hendrix Interview (1967)

This is the complete Meatball Fulton interview from December 1967 (see 'Hendrix Speaks' for full details).

THE INTERVIEW
CD CARD CCD 4082 (UK), 1994

Track: Jimi Hendrix Interview (1970)

Alias 'Crosstown Conversation', under a different title – in other words, Jimi, Mitch Mitchell and Noel Redding during the sup-

posed Experience reunion early in 1970. Brownie points for originality, though: this set is packaged as a greeting-card-with-free-CD, part of Baktabak's concerted effort to persuade every Hendrix fan in the universe to buy this interview at least once. Speaking of which...

INTROSPECTIVE
BAKTABAK CINT 5005 (UK), APRIL 1991

Tracks: Red House/Wake Up This Morning And Find Yourself Dead/Bleeding Heart/Jimi Hendrix Interview (1970)

It's that interview again – yes, Jimi, Noel and Mitch, February 1970 – but this time sequenced after three classic examples of the man in action. Or not, in fact, as the music comes from the chaotic Scene Club jam, and doesn't sound any better in this context than anywhere else.

INTROSPECTIVE/ THE WIND CRIES MARY
BAKTABAK CINT 25006 (UK), 1993

Tracks:
CD1: Red House/Wake Up This Morning And Find Yourself Dead/Bleeding Heart/Jimi Hendrix Interview (1970)
CD2: The Wind Cries Mary/Fire/Foxy Lady/May This Be Love

Brilliant, brilliant – give these boys a marketing diploma. 'Introspective' plainly didn't excite the masses, so Baktabak were left with a few spares on their hands. So they bought up bulk copies of an official Polydor CD single, featuring four original Experience recordings *circa* the making of their first album, and packaged the two together. Now why didn't I think of that?

JAMMING LIVE AT THE SCENE CLUB, N.Y.C.
REALISATION RLBC 012 (UK), 1994

Tracks: Wake Up This Morning And Find Yourself Dead/Outside Woman Blues/ Sunshine Of Your Love/Morrison's Lament/ Tomorrow Never Knows/Uranus Rock/Red House/Bleeding House

Proof that honesty sometimes is the best policy, even on the shadier side of the street. As you'll have gathered by now, the 1968 Scene Club jam is an inessential addition to any Hendrix collection. But you can't ask for much more than an album that comes clean about its contents from the start, admits that "the quality of the recording is not of today's high standard", and accurately comments that the music is "rough, but with the dynamism of Jimi's guitar to the fore". Only two major flaws: the cover photo shows Jimi playing right-handed, and the writer of The Beatles' 'Tomorrow Never Knows' is strangely listed as 'unknown'.

JIMI HENDRIX EXPERIENCE

ROCKSTARS IN CONCERT 6127092 (HOLLAND), 1992

Tracks: Hey Joe/Foxy Lady/Purple Haze/ Little Wing/Killing Floor/Voodoo Child (Slight Return)/Wild Thing/Fire/The Wind Cries Mary/Red House/The Burning Of The Midnight Lamp/Star Spangled Banner/Can You See Me?/Spanish Castle Magic

Before the lawyers managed to make some sense out of the different requirements and ramifications of copyright legislation across the European Community, CDs like this were ostensibly legal in Holland, and were imported into Britain as (semi-)legitimate releases. Don't try this at home, though, as the material on 'Jimi Hendrix Experience' is now firmly under the jurisdiction of the guitarist's estate. There are four sources for these tracks, in fact, and three of them have now been covered by official releases.

The earliest material comes from the Monterey festival in June 1967, available on 'Jimi Plays Monterey' ('Killing Floor', 'Wild Thing' and 'Can You See Me'). The first three tracks on the CD, plus 'Fire', 'The Wind Cries Mary' and 'The Burning Of The Midnight Lamp', are all from Stockholm on September 5, 1967 – a set reproduced in full on the 'Stages' box set.

That's also where you'll find the versions of 'Little Wing' and 'Red House' included here, as recorded by The Experience at the Olympia in Paris in January 1968. Finally, 'Voodoo Child (Slight Return)', 'Star Spangled Banner' and 'Spanish Castle Magic' all herald from another Stockholm show, this time on January 9, 1969. Those of you who've been drawing graphs of all this will remember that two further songs from that concert, plus those Stockholm 1967 tracks, appeared on the equally (legally) dubious offering, 'The Gold Collection'.

JIMI HENDRIX 1967: STANDING NEXT TO A MOUNTAIN

IF 6 WAS 9 JH01 (SWEDEN), C. 1991

Tracks: Swedish interviews
Sweden proved to be particularly receptive to The Jimi Hendrix Experience, and during their September 1967 European tour, the trio spent a week in towns like Gothenburg, Vasteras, Hogbö and Stockholm. This useful CD, packaged in a limited edition (1,000 copies) imitation tape box with two glossy photos, collects a variety of interview snippets from the tour, benefiting from a better command of the English language from the band's inquisitors than Jimi & Co. would have managed if they'd had to answer in Swedish.

JIMI HENDRIX 1970

DISCUSSION MERMAN 1983 (UK), 1991

Track: Interview with the Jimi Hendrix Experience (1970)
The Jimi Hendrix Experience in 1970, eh? I wonder if... oh, of course it is. As The Experience never recorded or played any gigs in 1970, this must be their brief, interview-only reunion in February of that year, when they were quizzed by journalist John Burks. 30 minutes of their encounter are available on several CDs already listed.

But wait, there's a bonus. This still isn't quite a complete document of the occasion, but at 65 minutes it's infinitely more generous than any of its rivals. It's also attractively packaged with some photos in a box – to the point where it's almost safe to recommend you buy this.

THE LAST EXPERIENCE

BESCOL CD-42 (ITALY), 1987

Tracks: Little Wing/Voodoo Child (Slight Return)/Room Full Of Mirrors/Fire/Purple Haze/Wild Thing/Bleeding Heart/The Sunshine Of Your Love/Room Full Of Mirrors/Bleeding Heart/Smashing Of Amps
The Last Experience: let me see, that must be the Denver Pop Festival on June 29, 1969, right? Well, no. This is our old friend, the Royal Albert Hall show from February, four months before the group exploded, complete

with the duplicated versions of 'Room Full Of Mirrors' and 'Bleeding Heart'. Check the listing for the 'Experience' CD on Bulldog to find out why this isn't an essential purchase.

NB: This CD was also released briefly on Galaxis 9006 under the title 'Experience'.

LIVE AT MONTEREY POP FESTIVAL
ITM MEDIA 960008 (ITALY), 1993

Tracks: Can You See Me?/Hey Joe/Purple Haze/The Wind Cries Mary/Killing Floor/Foxy Lady/Like A Rolling Stone/Rock Me, Baby/ Wild Thing

This is a strange one. The entire Hendrix set from this memorable, reputation-boosting performance in June 1967 is available on an official Polydor CD entitled 'Jimi Plays Monterey'. So how could a reputable UK distribution company like Koch International find themselves importing an Italian (supposedly, though clues suggest it's actually German) release duplicating the official release, without any mention of the Hendrix Estate, curator Alan Douglas or Polydor in the packaging? One for the legal boys to sort out, I guess. Anyway, there's no reason on earth to buy this: the official CD is cheaper and sounds better, with edits between

tracks that don't sound as if they were performed with rusty shears, and the songs presented in the right order.

MASTERPIECES
PULSAR PULS 008 (EUROPE), 1992

Tracks: Blues Blues/Night Life/Lime Lime/Psycho/Go Go Shoes/Bleeding Heart/Nobody Can Change Me/Sweet Thang/Bring My Baby Back/Good Feeling

The usual menu of rubbish: some low-protein Lonnie Youngblood, spiced with tasteless offcuts from the Scene Club. A masterpiece only in the cash-in stakes.

MORE EXPERIENCE
JIMCO JICK 89372 (JAPAN), 1994

Tracks: Little Wing/Voodoo Child (Slight Return)/Room Full Of Mirrors/Fire/Purple Haze/Wild Thing/Bleeding Heart

More Experience, more irrelevant duplication. As if countless CDs reissuing the Royal Albert Hall show from February 1969 weren't enough, Jimco just had to issue both the 'Experience' and 'More Experience' albums as originally issued in the early 70s. They were wasting their time, and so will you be if you buy this.

NEW YORK SESSIONS
TRADITIONAL LINE CD 1301 (GERMANY)

Tracks: Red House/Everything's Gonna Be Alright/Bleeding Heart/Tomorrow Never Knows/The Sunshine Of Your Love

You've already guessed: the Scene Club, which is in New York, so the title was accurate enough. Might be better packaged as 'Jim Morrison: The Drinking Session', though. Pointless.

NIGHT LIFE
THUNDERBOLT CDTB 075 (UK), APRIL 1990

Tracks: Good Feeling/Hot Trigger/Psycho/Come On Baby Part 1/Come On Baby Part 2/Night Life/You Got It/Woke Up This Morning/Tomorrow Never Knows Part 1/Bleeding Heart/Tomorrow Never Knows Part 2

Yet another collection of Lonnie Youngblood tracks ('Good Feeling' to 'You Got It', with only the two halves of 'Come On Baby' likely to feature Hendrix), plus four cuts from the Scene Club jam. Thunderbolt did it again a few weeks later with 'Free Spirit'.

PURPLE HAZE
SUCCESS 2101CD (GERMANY)

Tracks: Red House/Voodoo Child (Slight Return)/Bleeding Heart/Fire/Purple Haze/Room Full Of Mirrors/Smashing Of Amps/Wild Thing/The Sunshine Of Your Love/She's So Fine/Suspicious/Something You Got (check order)

'Red House' (thankfully edited) is from the Scene Club; the rest, bar the final three tracks which don't feature Hendrix anyway, is taken from the Albert Hall. It's all available elsewhere, cheaper and in better company.

PURPLE HAZE
ON STAGE CD 12010 (ITALY), 1993

Tracks: The Wind Cries Mary/The Burning Of The Midnight Lamp/Foxy Lady/Voodoo Child (Slight Return)/Killing Floor/Sgt. Pepper's Lonely Hearts Club Band/Hey Joe/The Sunshine Of Your Love/Little Wing/Fire/Red House/Purple Haze/Star Spangled Banner

This is nearly, but not quite, the same as the Dutch 'Jimi Hendrix Experience' release on the Rockstars In Concert label. It omits the Monterey tracks, replacing them with 'Sunshine Of Your Love' from the LA Forum in April 1969; and it features several extra tracks from Stockholm, both in 1967 and 1969. Also featured are the three familiar tracks from the Paris Olympia in 1968.

At budget price, which is the way it appeared in British stores in 1993, this is almost worth recommending as an introduction to the man's stage-work. But it is still in effect a bootleg in the UK, and only the turning of several blind eyes allowed it to go on open sale here in the first place.

PURPLE HAZE

JASREC EX-3012 (JAPAN), 1993

Tracks: Purple Haze/Hey Joe/Love Or Confusion/The Wind Cries Mary/Fire/Foxy Lady/Are You Experienced?/Spanish Castle Magic/Wait Until Tomorrow/Little Wing/ Castles Made Of Sand/One Rainy Wish/ Little Miss Lover/Bold As Love

Original Experience recordings, in the 127th permutation achieved by the Japanese. Marvellously irrelevant cover artwork, too.

PURPLE HAZE IN WOODSTOCK

ITM MEDIA 960004 (ITALY), APRIL 1993

Tracks: Getting My Heart Back Together Again (Hear My Train A-Comin')/Spanish Castle Magic/Red House/Lover Man/ Fire/Voodoo Child (Slight Return)/Star Spangled Banner/Purple Haze/A Minor Jam/Hey Joe

Another mysterious offering from ITM via the Koch International connection (see 'Live At Monterey Pop Festival'). It's appallingly packaged (it gets the date of the Woodstock festival wrong, for a start, and the front cover shot is actually from the Isle Of Wight), and its sound quality doesn't come close to matching the official ':Woodstock' CD.

Sadly, it's not simply a case of recommending the official disc, and leaving it at that. If we accept 'Purple Haze At Woodstock' as a legal release (though I don't, despite its appearance in major UK stores), then it does offer some advantages over the official set – namely its inclusion of 'Spanish Castle Magic', 'Lover Man' and 'Hey Joe', none of which has ever appeared on a 100% legal release. Which begs the question of why Alan Douglas and friends didn't issue the entire Hendrix set on their CD, instead of a reorganised, massively truncated selection.

PSYCHEDELIC VOODOO CHILE
REMEMBER 75053 (UK)

Tracks: Get That Feeling/How Would You Feel/Hush Now/No Business/Simon Says/ Gotta Have A New Dress/Strange Things/ Welcome Home/Love Love/Day Tripper/ Gloomy Monday/Fool For You Baby/Happy Birthday/Don't Accuse Me/Hornet's Nest/ Flashing/Odd Ball

Alias 'Early Classics' under an alternate title – the Curtis Knight studio sessions, in other words.

RED HOUSE
THE ENTERTAINERS CD 294 (ITALY), 1992

Tracks: House Burning Down/Voodoo Chile/Gypsy Eyes/Crosstown Traffic/Johnny B. Goode/Still Raining, Still Dreaming/The Burning Of The Midnight Lamp/Red House/All Along The Watchtower/Voodoo Child (Slight Return)

Here's one for the conspiracy theorists. The Ku Klux Klan and other White Supremacists from around the globe were appalled to discover that innocent white kids from Virginia to Vietnam had fallen under the sway of an evil black man touting the morals of drugs, sex and rock'n'roll. To break his spell, they organised a secret campaign of subversion – its object, the systematic destruction of Jimi Hendrix's stature as an artist.

Not convinced? Well, imagine the effect on innocent purchasers of this budget CD, labelled carefully 'Live Performances'. In fact, it contains eight tracks stolen from the 'Electric Ladyland' studio set, plus two from 'Hendrix In The West'. This is yet another skirting-the-edges-of-the-law compilation, issued under licence from nobody in particular. The record label lives up to its name by listing the second track as 'Woodoo Child' on the back cover. The two live cuts ('Red House' and 'Johnny B. Goode') are almost as good as Hendrix gets; likewise the studio stuff. Shame the sound quality is such crap. Now, prepared to consider the conspiracy idea?

16 GREATEST CLASSICS
BIG TIME 2615252 (GERMANY), MAY 1988

Tracks: Strange Things/Welcome Home/Day Tripper/Simon Says/Fool For You Baby/ Don't Accuse Me/Flashing/Odd Ball/ Hornet's Nest/Happy Birthday/ WhoaEch/ Sweet Thang/Voice In The Wind/Bring My

Baby Back/Good Times/Psycho

Not quite the right title, perhaps. Maybe they should have tried '16 Tracks Most Likely To Bring Jimi Into Disrepute'. Doesn't have the same ring, I agree, but it has accuracy on its side. This is a sad collection of Curtis Knight tracks (10 in all), Lonnie Youngblood irrelevancies (five, with only a couple of them featuring Hendrix) and one mistitled relic from that damned jam at the Scene Club. One for the Trade Descriptions Act – unless you're prepared to believe that someone at Big Time really thinks these are Hendrix's 16 greatest classics...

SPECIAL COLLECTION
JASREC GRN-52 (JAPAN), 1993

Tracks: Purple Haze/Hey Joe/Love Or Confusion/The Wind Cries Mary/Fire/Foxy Lady/Are You Experienced?/Spanish Castle Magic/Wait Until Tomorrow/Little Wing/ Castles Made Of Sand/One Rainy Wish/Little Miss Lover/Bold As Love

'Special' is one of those words like 'exclusive' that usually means the exact opposite of its dictionary definition. In this case, it's best defined as "another random selection of Jimi

Hendrix Experience studio tracks available in far more sensible surroundings elsewhere". This release is particularly pointless, as it duplicates another Japanese CD, 'Purple Haze'.

SPOTLIGHT
SONET SPCD-8 (UK)

Tracks: Little Wing/Voodoo Child (Slight Return)/Room Full Of Mirrors/Fire/Purple Haze/Bleeding Heart/The Sunshine Of Your Love/Room Full Of Mirrors/Bleeding Heart/Smashing Of Amps

Another pointless repackage of Bulldog's 'Experience' album from the Albert Hall show in February 1969 – again. Don't suppose the title could be any attempt to cash in on the official 'Footlights', could it?

STRANGE THINGS
SUCCESS 2171CD (GERMANY)

Tracks: Flashing/Hornet's Nest/Don't Accuse Me/Simon Says/Day Tripper/ Welcome Home/Strange Things/ Odd Ball/All I Want/ Whoaech/Down Mean Blues/Monday Morning Blues/Bring My Baby Back/ Suspicious/Good Times/Hot Trigger/ Psycho/Good Feeling

Strange things indeed, mama: if you recognise this concept, it's because you've just been reading about Big Time's '16 Greatest Classics', which has an almost identical track listing – comprised of Knight, Youngblood and (one) Scene Club recordings. At least they didn't call it '18 Greatest Classics'.

SUPER SELECTION
ECHO EVC 336 (JAPAN), 1994

Tracks: Purple Haze/One Rainy Wish/Bold As Love/Little Wing/Spanish Castle Magic/She's So Fine/You've Got Me Floating/Are You Experienced?/May This Be Love/Foxy Lady/Little Miss Lover/The Wind Cries Mary/Love Or Confusion/Third Stone From The Sun/Fire/Manic Depression/Hey Joe/I Don't Live Today

I can picture it now: Echo's track compiler comes up with his choice of Hendrix studio recordings for yet another CD. His wife runs her eyes down the list, and cries out, "Super selection, darling". "Eureka," screams Mr Echo, and so 'Super Selection' it is. Tragically, this scenario fails to explain why the front cover has, not a picture of Hendrix, but a Beverly Hills T-shirt.

SUPERSESSION
JIMCO JICK 89214 (JAPAN), 1993

Tracks: Red House/I'm Gonna Leave This Town; Everything's Gonna Be Alright/Bleeding Heart/Tomorrow Never Knows/Outside Woman Blues; The Sunshine Of Your Love

"Live with Johnny Winter and Jim Morrison," cries the cover of this 147th reissue of the Scene Club jam. Shame that Johnny Winter was in Texas that night, and that Jim's major contribution was inventing four-letter words in a drunken stupor. Some dreadful records have been credited with the 'supersession' tag since Al Kooper invented the concept back in 1968, but few of them have been as dire as this.

THE VERY BEST OF JIMI HENDRIX
MILLENIUM MILCD 03 (ITALY), 1994

Tracks: Purple Haze/Voodoo Child (Slight Return)/The Sunshine Of Your Love/Voodoo Child (Slight Return)/Experiencing The Blues (Catfish Blues)/Killing Floor/Can You Please Crawl Out Your Window/Hey Joe

Not exactly the very best, but there have been worse albums than this purporting to offer

Hendrix's finest moments. Keen readers will recognise this as the second half of the 'Gold Collection' double-CD, which featured unofficially liberated recordings from live shows in 1967 and 1969.

Featured here, then, are three cuts from the LA Forum in April 1969; 'Experiencing The Blues' (alias 'Catfish Blues') from Holland in November 1967; 'Killing Floor' and 'Hey Joe' from two different Stockholm shows in January 1969; and 'Can You Please Crawl Out Your Window' from an errant Radio One session in October 1967. Even allowing for its sonic deficiencies, this is worth investigating if you find it cheap enough (like £6), but don't tell the lawyers, OK?

VOICE IN THE WIND
TRACE 0401022 (HOLLAND), 1993

Tracks: *Good Times/Voices/Suspicious/ Whipper/Bessie Mae/Soul Food/Voice In The Wind/Free Spirit/Good Feeling/Hot Trigger/Psycho/Come On Baby Part 1/ Come On Baby Part 2/Night Life/You Got It/Woke Up This Morning/Tomorrow Never Knows Part 1/ Bleeding Heart/Tomorrow Never Knows Part 2*

This time the voice in the wind says: seen this, heard this, bought this, felt sick. That's because the diet – Lonnie Youngblood trash plus extracts from the Scene Club jam – is as stodgy and nutritious as eating concrete. And you can always use concrete to build yourself a garden path.

VOICES
PILZ 448221-2 (GERMANY), 1993

Tracks: *Good Times/Voices/Suspicious/ Whipper/Goodbye Bessie Mae/Soul Food/Voice In The Wind/Free Spirit.*
Not just one voice, this time, but a whole chorus of them – all saying, don't buy this CD, it's more of that Lonnie Youngblood rubbish. Quite right too. For the same sorry song selection under a different title, see 'Free Spirit'.

VOICES IN THE WIND
THUNDERBOLT CDTBD 001 (UK), JUNE 1988

Tracks featuring Hendrix: *Good Times/ Voices/Suspicious/Whipper/Goodbye Bessie Mae/Soul Food/Voice In The Wind/ Free Spirit*
'Voice In The Wind', 'Voices', 'Voices In The

Wind' – you can see how this is building up. This was our old buddy, the 'Free Spirit' album, reissued as part of a double-CD with an equally unexciting Tina Turner disc.

VOLUME 1/VOLUME 2
WISEPACK LECDD 603 (UK), 1992

Tracks:
CD1: Good Feeling/Go Go Shoes/Bring My Baby Back/Psycho/Come On Baby/Blues Blues/Sweet Thang/Lime Lime/Peoples Peoples/Whoa Ech/Night Life/Nobody Can Change Me/You Got It
CD2: Red House/Woke Up This Morning/ Bleeding Heart/Morrison's Lament/ Tomorrow Never Knows/Uranus Rock/ Outside Woman Blues/The Sunshine Of Your Love

Living proof that two wrongs make a crime, this misbegotten set manages not only to rip off the fans, but to do it twice. First, its musical contents are crap (the Lonnie Youngblood tracks plus the Scene Club, as usual); secondly, it repeats about half the first CD on the second CD, albeit attempting to disguise the fact by using two different sets of titles for the same songs.

Now, you try and convince me that Wisepack didn't notice, or that they thought it was just what the fans wanted. Any company acting with such flagrant disregard for the public deserves to go out of business, but what's upsetting is the thought that a 14-year-old might buy this as their introduction to Hendrix (bargain price, two CDs for around eight quid) and vow never to listen to one of his records again. Shameless exploitation.

WOKE UP THIS MORNING AND FOUND MYSELF DEAD
RED LIGHTNIN' RLCD 0068 (UK), NOVEMBER 1986

Tracks: Red House/I'm Gonna Leave This Town; Everything's Gonna Be Alright/ Bleeding Heart/Tomorrow Never Knows/ Outside Woman Blues; The Sunshine Of Your Love

In the beginning there was a bootleg LP called 'Sky High', which is a fairly exact description of most of the participants of this jam session at (pause for fanfare) the Scene Club. Then in 1980, blues specialists Red Lightnin' took the plunge and released an annotated 'official' album of the sorry proceedings. Well, good luck to them: it was probably worth issuing once. But since then, every dodgy record label in Europe has had at least one shot at these recordings, and many thousands have fallen prey to the obscene mumblings of Jim Morrison and the below-par guitar exploits of Jimi Hendrix.

If anyone's entitled to release this set on CD, it's Red Lightnin', but the same material is now available more cheaply elsewhere – notably on Castle's 'Black And White Blues', to which you are recommended instead.

SECTION 4
GUESTAPPEARANCES

EIRE APPARENT
SUNRISE

LP RELEASE: BUDDAH 203 021 (UK), MAY 1969

CD RELEASE: SEQUEL NEXCD 199 (UK), FEBRUARY 1992

Tracks featuring Hendrix: Rock'n'Roll Band/Yes I Need Someone/The Clown/Mr Guy Fawkes/Someone Is Sure (To Want You)/Morning Glory/Magic Carpet/Captive In The Sun/Let Me Stay

Why did Jimi produce and play on almost an entire album of material by an otherwise unknown Irish rock band? Because they were being handled by his managers, Mike Jeffery and Chas Chandler. Hendrix contributed to their 'Rock'n'Roll Band' single and Sunrise album, both of which are highly enjoyable 1968 pop-rock, with some characteristically flamboyant guitar touches: sadly, his involvement failed to boost the band's sales.

THE ISLEY BROTHERS
THE ISLEY BROTHERS:
THE COMPLETE UA RECORDINGS

EMI CDP 7-95203-2 (US), 1991

The sleeve-notes to this album suggest that Hendrix probably played guitar on two tracks recorded on January 14, 1964, called 'The Basement' and 'Conch'. Sadly, Jimi didn't actually meet the Isleys until March 1964...

THE ISLEY BROTHERS STORY
VOLUME 1: ROCKIN' SOUL

RHINO R2 70908 (USA), 1991

Tracks featuring Hendrix: Testify Part 1/Testify Part 2/The Last Girl/Move Over And Let Me Dance

These Isley/Hendrix collaborations are authentic, however. 'Testify' was a double-sided single in 1964, the first release on the Isleys' own T-Neck label – and the last, at least until 1969. It's easy to see why it didn't sell: it was groundbreaking music, which came close to pioneering psychedelic soul four years too early. These are the first recordings that contain recognisable Hendrix guitar licks, and it's satisfying that they would be memorable tracks whether or not Jimi had played on them.

The other two songs here, cut during later sessions, aren't quite so thrilling, but they're still state of the art crossover R&B for 1964. Jimi also performed on two other Isley Brothers tracks, as yet unavailable on CD: 'Looking For A Love' and 'Have You Ever Been Disappointed'.

TIMOTHY LEARY
YOU CAN BE ANYONE THIS TIME AROUND

LP RELEASE: DOUGLAS 1 (USA), APRIL 1970
CD RELEASE: UFO BFTP 006 (UK), NOVEMBER 1991

Track featuring Hendrix: Live And Let Live
LSD guru Timothy Leary persuaded John Lennon to write him a campaign song for a planned assault on the governorship of California. Then Leary went to prison, and Lennon turned the song into a Beatles single, 'Come Together'. Also involved in the project

to create Leary anthems was Jimi Hendrix, whose jam with Stephen Stills, John Sebastian and Buddy Miles – taped by Douglas purely to document the session, rather than with any particular end in mind – was overdubbed with spoken-word extracts from the would-be governor, while he was in jail. Legend has it that the song the musicians were jamming around for 25 minutes – with Jimi on bass, not guitar – was Joni Mitchell's 'Woodstock', which wasn't actually written until August 1969, three months after the apparent date of this session.

LIGHTNIN' ROD
DORIELLA DU FONTAINE

RESTLESS 72663-2 (US), 1992

Tracks featuring Hendrix: Doriella Du Fontaine (Radio Edit)/Doriella Du Fontaine (instrumental)/Doriella Du Fontaine
Alan Douglas was producing the proto-rap group The Last Poets in 1969, when group member Lightnin' Rod cut this devilish piece of speech, part of a suite of 'Jail Toasts' – a clear precursor of the black music mainstream of the late Eighties and Nineties. Buddy Miles and Jimi Hendrix jammed behind

him, and the track might have ruffled a few industry feathers back in 1970. But it wasn't released until 1984, by which time it was little more than a historic curio. The CD release takes the basic track and subjects it to a remix and an edit.

LITTLE RICHARD
LITTLE RICHARD AND JIMI HENDRIX
CLASSIC ROCK CDCD 1108 (ITALY), 1993

Tracks featuring Hendrix: none
Jimi did record one session as a member of Little Richard's band, but despite its title, this CD has none of those cuts on it.

THE LITTLE RICHARD COLLECTION
CASTLE CCSCD 227 (UK), 1989

Tracks featuring Hendrix: I Don't Know What You've Got But It's Got Me/Dancin' All Around The World
The full list of Hendrix's cameos with Little Richard runs to both tracks – and they're both featured on this budget CD. Little Richard is sporadically wonderful on this disc, Hendrix hardly audible.

PEARLS OF THE PAST
WPC KLM CD 004 (HOLLAND), 1994

Track featuring Hendrix: Dancin' All Around The World
Just one of the Hendrix/Richard collaborations features on this disc.

ROCK'N'ROLL SPECIAL
PHONO-MUSIC CD926 (GERMANY)

The contents of this disc couldn't be confirmed: check above for the details of the two songs to watch out for.

LOVE
FALSE START
LP RELEASE: BLUE THUMB BTS 22 (USA), DECEMBER 1970
CD RELEASE: MCA MCAD 22029 (USA), 1990

Track featuring Hendrix: The Everlasting First
Jimi Hendrix and Arthur Lee first collaborated in early 1965, when Lee produced and Hendrix played on a one-off single by an artist called Rosa Lee Brooks. Sadly, the coupling of 'My Diary'/'Utee' is only available on bootleg.
The underground market also promised in 1989 to bring us an album called 'The Jimi And Arthur Experience' – supposedly releasing for

the first time a long session the two men may or may not have staged in March 1970. Various song titles have been bandied about down the years, but the only confirmed collaboration cut at that time was 'The Everlasting First', issued on Love's 'False Start' album in late 1970, and also as a single at the same time.

JAYNE MANSFIELD
JAYNE MANSFIELD
LEGEND CD 6008 (GERMANY), 1994

Tracks featuring Hendrix: Suey/As The Clouds Drift By

During his brief sojourn at Ed Chalpin's PPX stable with Curtis Knight, Hendrix was invited to perform on a single by actress/pin-up Jayne Mansfield. 'Suey', which features brief flourishes of recognisable Hendrix licks, was issued as a single; 'As The Clouds Drift By' from the same session was its flipside, and Chalpin claims that Jimi played all the instruments of the session. It doesn't sound like it.

MCGOUGH & MCGEAR
MCGOUGH & MCGEAR
LP RELEASE: PARLOPHONE PCS 7047 (UK), APRIL 1968
CD RELEASE: EMI CDP 7 91877 2 (UK), 1989

Tracks featuring Hendrix: So Much/Ex Art Student

McGough and McGear were Roger McGough (famous Liverpool poet) and Mike McCartney (brother of Paul). The Beatle connection, plus their involvement with the hit comedy/poetry/music group The Scaffold, helped them get a deal for a duo album – an amusing excursion into comedy and tragedy, aided by superstar friends.

Jimi played on three tracks during the January 1968 sessions, one of which remains unissued. The other two appeared on the CD reissue in 1989, and 'Ex Art Student' is actually a fine slice of UK late 60s pop.

STEPHEN STILLS
STEPHEN STILLS

LP RELEASE: ATLANTIC 2401 004 (UK), NOVEMBER 1970
CD RELEASE: ATLANTIC 7202-2 (USA)

Track featuring Hendrix: Old Times Good Times

Hendrix and Buffalo Springfield/CSNY multi-instrumentalist Stephen Stills first met at the Monterey Pop Festival, and jammed several times over the next three years. Stills actually took part in some Hendrix studio sessions, and can be heard (for example) on 'My Friend' from 'The Cry Of Love'.

When Stills was assembling his first studio album in March 1970 at Olympic Studios in London, Hendrix was a natural choice for a cameo appearance. His contribution, 'Old Times Good Times', was actually overshadowed by the Stills/Clapton collaboration which followed it on the album, but since 1970 Stills has regularly claimed (a) that he has numerous other tracks from the same session, notably one called 'White Nigger', and (b) that he is about to release them. He was last quizzed on the subject in 1992, when he was sticking to both stories.